God's

Provision For All

A DEFENSE OF GOD'S GOODNESS

Leighton Flowers, D.Min

Trinity Academic Press

God's Provision for All

A Defense of God's Goodness

By Leighton C. Flowers, D.Min

Director of Evangelism &

Apologetics for Texas Baptists

Contributions by:

Eric Kemp

Billy Wendeln

Matthew Chisholm

Special thanks to Marlene Weeks, copyeditor

ISBN-13: 978-1-7328963-0-7
ISBN-10: 1-7328963-0-5

Dedicated to

My Grandfather
Harlin "Rusty" Hampton

For demonstrating to me how God provides for
the needs of others through His children.

My Parents
Chuck and Mary Flowers

For demonstrating to me the unconditional love of
God long before I understood it for myself.

My Wife
Laura Flowers

For demonstrating to me that love is best
recognized through patience and self-sacrifice.

My Children
Caden, Esther, Cooper & Colson

For demonstrating to me that love has not fully
matured until you are willing to let go and allow it
to walk on its own.

Table of Contents

Introduction

I f there is one presupposition a student of the Bible should bring to any text, it is this: Our God is good and always does what is right. But, what does it really mean to say, "He is good?" By what standard does one determine what is right? Is there an objective measure of goodness or rightness by which mankind can determine within themselves whether or not God is a good Creator rather than some tyrannical deity? Who is man, after all, to judge the goodness or rightness of the One who spoke all of us and our universe into being?

The only measure of good (as opposed to bad) or right (as opposed to wrong) by which people can make such assessments must come from the source, God. He does not disappoint. From the very beginning, God has revealed His character to mankind, which is the standard of good and evil, right and wrong.

The purpose of this book is to demonstrate, through the Scriptures, that God is genuinely and recognizably good. By "recognizably good" I mean that His goodness is evident and demonstrable, not just an empty platitude we say because we feel that we must.

If your boss is a mean and vindictive slave driver and someone asks you what you think of him when you know he is listening, are you going to be honest or are you going to say what you know he would want to hear for fear of retribution?

It appears that many Christians, even those who believe some seemingly distasteful things about God, affirm His goodness based on fear or obligation rather than on what they think is true about His character as demonstrated by His choices and actions. Allow me to illustrate this point by telling you about my grandfather, Harlin "Rusty" Hampton.

Prior to his passing, my grandfather was one of the most influential people in my life. He was a generous man who consistently provided for those in need. He lived his life by the principle that "everything not given is lost" and those who knew him noticed. I recall on many occasions my grandpa pulling onto the side of the road to help a stranded motorist. Having served as a machinist during the second World War, there was rarely an engine he could not fix. Though not a man of great wealth, he was constantly giving away tools, furniture or even vehicles to those he felt needed them more.

One year, long before I was born, my grandpa and his family went on vacation only to return and find that their house had burned to the ground due to faulty wiring. While the insurance covered the cost of the home, it did not cover all the possessions they had lost in the fire. When news of my grandpa's loss spread throughout the community many people began showing up to return items he had given away, often accompanied by a few more much needed essentials.

Before long a new house was filled by many of the very things my grandpa had previously given away. This is why he also taught his children and grandchildren the principle that "everything not given is lost."

"This is not only true of our possessions, which we can't take with us when we die," he explained. "It is also true of our very lives. Every life not given to the Lord is lost forever."

At my grandpa's funeral I recall many people who said to me, "Your grandpa was a good man," but they did not stop there as if to merely give an empty platitude to comfort me in my loss. No, they went on to tell a story of how my beloved grandpa had provided for them or their family in a time of need. In other words, they demonstrated to me how they *recognized* that Rusty was a good man. People *recognized* my grandpa's character as good because he provided for others in their time of need.

Can we all agree that a *recognizably good* person provides for the needs of others, not because they have to, but because of their good and benevolent character? I believe that is a fair and reasonable conclusion, don't you? If so, then what would it mean to call God "*recognizably good?*"

I believe we recognize our God as good, especially as revealed to us through Christ, because He provides for all who are in need. He does not make His provisions because He has to, but because of who He is. He is a good and benevolent God!

WHAT DOES THE SCRIPTURE SAY ABOUT HIS GOODNESS?

After He created man and woman in His own image, the Scripture says: "God saw everything that He had made, and behold, it was very good" (Gen. 1:31). God made people "very good." He did not mess up when He made humanity. God did not create us broken; incapable of determining right from wrong. He did not create us as selfish, sinful wretches who can do nothing more than rebel in hatred. One of the implications of being made in the *image of God* is the ability to know God's standard of right and wrong.

However, the question becomes: how can creatures who were created "very good" commit the heinous evil that begins almost immediately? God created humans with the ability to make real choices which allows for such evil. As C.S. Lewis rightly explained,

God created things which had free will. That means creatures which can go either wrong or right. Some people think they can imagine a creature which was free but had no possibility of going wrong; I cannot. If a thing is free to be good it is also free to be bad. And free will is what has made evil possible. Why,

4

then, did God give them free will? Because free will, though it makes evil possible, is also the only thing that makes possible any love or goodness or joy worth having. A world of automata—of creatures that worked like machines—would hardly be worth creating. The happiness which God designs for His higher creatures is the happiness of being freely, voluntarily united to Him and to each other in an ecstasy of love and delight compared with which the most rapturous love between a man and a woman on this earth is mere milk and water. And for that they must be free... If God thinks this state of war in the universe a price worth paying for free will—that is, for making a live world in which creatures can do real good or harm and something of real importance can happen, instead of a toy world which only moves when He pulls the strings—then we may take it, it is worth paying.[1]

God created people with the moral capacity to freely choose between good and evil. Remember the one presupposition all should bring to any text is that our God is good. Therefore, it should not be concluded that God, or His decrees, are the source of this morally evil choice of Adam and Eve to rebel. The apostle John confirmed this when he wrote:

---

[1] C.S. Lewis, *Mere Christianity* (New York: Simon & Schuster, 1996), 52-53.

1 John 2:16: For all that is in the world, the lust of the flesh and the lust of the eyes and the boastful pride of life, is not from the Father, but is from the world.

Therefore, no Bible believer should ever imply that the source of mankind's evil desire is God, or His decree. Mankind alone is responsible for their desires and choices to sin against Him. God's sovereign choice to create people with the moral ability to do good or evil cannot be conflated with instilling in mankind a particular and unavoidable evil desire or inclination.

THE KNOWLEDGE OF GOOD AND EVIL

The name of the forbidden tree placed in the garden with Adam and Eve should not go unnoticed. It was aptly named "the tree of the knowledge of good and evil" (Gen. 2:17). That phrase implies fallen humanity has the ability to discern for themselves the difference between good and evil, what is right or wrong.

To eat of the "tree of the knowledge of good and evil" was a rejection of God as the perfect Creator who knows what is best for His creation. So, it happened when Adam and Eve chose to rebel, God concluded in Genesis 3:22, "Behold, the man has become like one of Us, knowing good and evil." Thus, sin did not result in less knowledge or less understanding, but more. The fall introduced the ability to know the difference between both right and wrong. The Bible gives us no clear indication that humanity lost their ability to choose between right and wrong due to this fall. In fact, it seems to be quite the opposite.

In Genesis 4, the Lord speaks to Cain saying, "If you do well, will not your countenance be lifted up? And if you do not do well, sin is crouching at the door; and its desire is for you, but you must master it." This implies that it is Cain's responsibility to choose between what is right and wrong.

Now, if he does choose what is right does that mean he has merited justification before God? Of course not! Cain's brother, Abel, while making the morally right decision did not earn or merit his salvation on the basis of that decision. If he did, then there would have been no reason for Christ to atone for his sin. We cannot conflate mankind's ability to recognize and respond positively to God and His truth with an ability to atone for sin or merit grace.

All people, everywhere and in all times, since the fall, have an innate knowledge of both good and evil. In other words, all people naturally understand the difference between what is morally right and wrong. This is the conscience expounded upon by the apostle Paul:

Romans 2:15: ...the Law written in their hearts, their conscience bearing witness and their thoughts alternately accusing or else defending them.

This means when someone lies, murders, steals, cheats or sins in any number of ways, they innately know they have not done what is right. Because of this innate knowledge created within mankind by their Maker everyone can, on some level, know that which is good, just, fair and right about the One who made them.

RECOGNIZABLY GOOD

Some may conclude that mankind's fallen and sinful condition prevents anyone from making sound judgments about God's character and actions, but if this is so, then on what basis can anyone believe God is actually good as opposed to evil? As C.S. Lewis so eloquently stated,

> If God's moral judgment differs from ours so that our 'black' may be His 'white', we can mean nothing by calling Him good; for to say 'God is good', while asserting that His goodness is wholly other than ours, is really only to say 'God is we know not what'. And an utterly unknown quality in God cannot give us moral grounds for loving or obeying Him. If He is not (in our sense) 'good' we shall obey, if at all, only through fear — and should be equally ready to obey an omnipotent Fiend [all-powerful demon].[2]

In other words, people have no basis on which to worship God as a *recognizably good* Creator unless there is

---

[2] C.S. Lewis, *The Problem of Pain* (New York, NY: HarperCollinsPublishers, 1940), 19.

a foundation on which to rest their understanding of goodness. That foundation is what God reveals in creation (Rom. 1:19-20), writes upon the hearts of His image bearers (Rom. 2:15), and confirms by His Word (Rom. 3:25-26). Creation, the Messiah, and His gospel message all scream of God's praiseworthiness and establishes once and for all time what is truly right, noble and *good*.

WHAT DOES THE BIBLE REVEAL ABOUT GOD'S CHARACTER?

God is righteous. He has perfect moral character. He is recognizably loving, compassionate, longsuffering, holy, just, merciful, gracious, impartial, and sovereign. God's character (nature) is directly linked to His plan and purpose for mankind. One cannot separate character from behavior, not even as it is related to God, because this is what the Bible teaches (1 Peter 1:14-16).

God is holy, holy, holy

The use of repetition in Hebrew writing was a means of emphasis. God is thrice holy because there are none above Him.

Isaiah 6:3: And one called out to another and said, "Holy, holy, holy is the LORD of hosts, the whole earth is full of his glory."

1 Peter 1:16: Because it is written, "YOU SHALL BE HOLY, FOR I AM HOLY."

9

Revelation 4:8: And the four living creatures, each one of them having six wings, are full of eyes around and within; and day and night they do not cease to say, "HOLY, HOLY, HOLY is THE LORD GOD, THE ALMIGHTY, WHO WAS AND WHO IS AND WHO IS TO COME."

Ezekiel 39:7: My holy name I will make known in the midst of my people Israel; and I will not let My holy name be profaned anymore. And the nations will know that I am the LORD, the Holy One in Israel.

God is gracious

Though we are fallen, God gives us blessings despite our sinful ways; because He loves us, He gives us grace, unmerited favor.

James 4:6: But he gives us more grace. That is why Scripture says: "God opposes the proud, but shows favor to the humble."

John 1:16: For of His fullness we have all received, grace upon grace.

Titus 3:7: So that being justified by his grace we would be made heirs according to the hope of eternal life.

Hebrews 4:16: Therefore let us draw near with confidence to the throne of grace, so that we may receive mercy and find grace to help in time of need.

God is good

By God's nature we know goodness. He is the objective standard by which we can judge right and wrong.

Mark 10:18: And Jesus said to him, "Why do you call Me good? No one is good except God alone."

John 10:11: I am the good shepherd. The good shepherd lays down his life for the sheep.

Psalm 136:1: Give thanks to the LORD, for he is good. His steadfast love endures forever.

Psalm 119:68: You are good and do good; Teach me Your statutes.

Psalm 143:10: Teach me to do Your will, For You are my God; Let your good Spirit lead me on level ground.

God embodies goodness; His actions are the antithesis of evil. God, in His goodness, always has our best interests at heart. God genuinely desires for us to be free from wickedness and dedicated to good.

Mankind, in our fallen nature, does not deserve God's blessing. Through His omniscience, and in keeping with His holy, good, and loving character, God has nevertheless predetermined a gracious plan to redeem us from sin. Through His work, He provided us the gift of His Son, the Lord Jesus Christ.

God is love, and His ways are loving

His enduring love is the reason we have been given the opportunity for salvation. It is because He loves us that we have received the truth of who He is and what He has done.

1 John 4:8: The one who does not love does not know God, for God is love.

1 John 4:16: We have come to know and have believed the love which God has for us. God is love, and the one who abides in love abides in God, and God abides in him.

1 John 4:9-11: By this the love of God was manifested in us, that God has sent His only begotten Son into the world so that we might live through him. In this is love, not that we have loved God, but that He loved us and sent His Son to be the propitiation for our sins. Beloved, if God so loved us, we also ought to love one another.

John 3:16: For God so loved the world, that He gave His only begotten Son, that whoever believes in Him will not perish, but have eternal life.

John 16:27: For the Father himself loves you, because you have loved Me and have believed that I came forth from the Father.

1 John 3:1: See how great a love the Father has bestowed on us, that we should be called children of God; and such we are. For this reason the world does not know us, because it did not know Him.

God is full of patience, compassion, and mercy

God has not hastened the day of His wrath. Instead, He has patiently waited so that man may seek Him and hopefully find Him. He is never far off. He has compassion for the lost, and His desire is that they should accept the grace He has offered so that they may receive mercy.

Exodus 34:6: Then the Lord passed by in front of him and proclaimed, "The LORD, the LORD GOD, compassionate and gracious, slow to anger, and abounding in lovingkindness and truth."

Psalm 86:15: But you, O Lord, are a God merciful and gracious, Slow to anger and abundant in lovingkindness and truth.

Psalm 78:38: But He, being compassionate, forgave their iniquity and did not destroy them; And often He restrained His anger and did not arouse His wrath.

Joel 2:13: Return to the LORD your God, for he is gracious and compassionate, slow to anger and abounding in love, and he relents from sending calamity.

God is perfectly fair and just

God does not distinguish between people groups, races, genders, ages, or any other contrasting feature among men. He is not partial, and thus He is fair. He is not partial, and thus He can be just.

Romans 2:11: For there is no partiality with God.

Acts 10:34: Then Peter began to speak: "I now realize how true it is that God does not show favoritism."

Ephesians 6:9: And masters, treat your slaves the same way. Do not threaten them, since you know that he who is both their Master and yours is in heaven, and there is no favoritism with him.

James 2:1: My brothers and sisters, believers in our glorious Lord Jesus Christ must not show favoritism.

James 2:8-9: If, however, you are fulfilling the royal law according to the Scripture, "you shall love your neighbor as yourself," you are doing well. But if you show partiality, you are committing sin and are convicted by the law as transgressors.

God's judgment is perfect

Because we understand perfection through His nature, we understand that His ways and His judgment are perfect. He is not perfect by some higher standard. He is perfect because He is.

Psalm 9:8: And He will judge the world in righteousness; He will execute judgment for the peoples with equity.

Psalm 98:9: For He is coming to judge the earth; He will judge the world with righteousness, And the peoples with equity.

Jeremiah 17:10: I, the Lord, search the heart, I test the mind, Even to give to each man according to his ways, According to the results of his deeds.

Jeremiah 11:20: But, O LORD of hosts, who judges righteously, Who tries the feelings and the heart, Let me see Your vengeance on them, For to You I have committed my cause.

Genesis 18:25: Far be it from You to do such a thing, to slay the righteous with the wicked, so that the righteous and the wicked are treated alike. Far be it from You! Shall not the Judge of all the earth deal justly?

2 Timothy 4:8: In the future there is laid up for me the crown of righteousness, which the Lord, the righteous Judge, will award me on that day; and not only to me, but also to all who have loved His appearing.

God desires all to be saved

Because He is loving, impartial, and fair, God has made a way for all to be saved. He desires that all come to the saving knowledge of the truth so that they may share in the mercy that was bought with Christ's blood.

1 Timothy 2:4: …who wants all people to be saved and to come to a knowledge of the truth.

2 Peter 3:9: The Lord is not slow about His promise, as some count slowness, but is patient toward you, not wishing for any to perish but for all to come to repentance.

Matthew 18:14: In the same way your Father in heaven is not willing that any of these little ones should perish.

John 12:47: If anyone hears my sayings and does not keep them, I do not judge him; for I did not come to judge the world, but to save the world.

Ezekiel 18:23: Do I take any pleasure in the death of the wicked? declares the Sovereign LORD. Rather, am I not pleased when they turn from their ways and live?

God is sovereign

Many people have mistaken sovereignty with absolute control; unless God absolutely controls everything, He is not completely sovereign. This is a twisted definition, and tends to define God as a celestial puppet master. One scholar explains,

If you look up sovereignty in the dictionary you'll not find *control* in the definition—nor even as a synonym in a thesaurus… Sovereignty means *rightful authority*. A dictionary gives *supreme rank* as one definition, and a thesaurus lists *jurisdiction* and *dominion* as synonyms. The doctrine of God's sovereignty tells us God is the rightful ruler of the universe. He has legitimate claim to lordship. His government is just. In fact, justice is defined as His rule. God's sovereignty doesn't tell us whether God does in fact rule—just that he ought to, and that we should acknowledge his rule and obey it. [3]

Job 42:2: I know that You can do all things, And that no purpose of Yours can be thwarted.

Psalms 33:11: But the plans of the LORD stand firm forever, the purposes of His heart through all generations.

Psalm 103:19: The LORD has established His throne in the heavens, And His sovereignty rules over all.

Proverbs 16:4: The LORD has made everything for its own purpose, Even the wicked for the day of evil.

---

[3] One Reformed author warns against the growing tendency of misusing the word *sovereignty*: "What does it mean to say that God is sovereign? The refrain has become so common, almost clichéd, in Reformed writing and preaching that it sometimes slips away from the reader or listener without lodging meaning in the mind. Worse, we typically hear the phrase to mean something it doesn't. When Christians affirm that 'God is sovereign,' they often mean 'God is in control.' The problem is that the English word sovereignty does not mean control. The U. S. government is sovereign within American territory, but that doesn't mean the government controls everything within American borders or causes all that happens." Paul D. Miller, "Is 'Sovereign' the Best Descriptor for God?" *The Gospel Coalition.* Quote taken from: https://www.thegospelcoalition.org/article/is-sovereign-the-best-descriptor-for-god/ [date accessed 12/15/18].

Proverbs 19:21: Many plans are in a man's heart, But the counsel of the LORD will stand.

Isaiah 25:1: O LORD, you are my God; I will exalt You, I will give thanks to your name; For You have worked wonders, Plans formed long ago, with perfect faithfulness.

Isaiah 46:9-11: Remember the former things, those of long ago; I am God, and there is no other; I am God, and there is none like me. I make known the end from the beginning, from ancient times, what is still to come. I say, "My purpose will stand, and I will do all that I please." From the east I summon a bird of prey; from a far-off land, a man to fulfill my purpose. What I have said, that I will bring about; what I have planned, that I will do.

Jeremiah 32:19: Great are your purposes and mighty are your deeds. Your eyes are open to the ways of all mankind; you reward each person according to their conduct and as their deeds deserve.

Everything under creation falls under God's power, influence, and authority. God rules it all. There is no one that can thwart His purpose and that purpose includes a creation with responsible creatures.

God is our example

As the creator who is above all things, He is our absolute standard. We are told in Scripture to consider

18

His ways and imitate Him. Knowing God leads to fearing God. The fear of God is the beginning of wisdom.

1 Samuel 12:24: Only fear the LORD and serve Him in truth with all your heart; for consider what great things He has done for you.

Job 23:15: Therefore, I would be dismayed at His presence; When I consider, I am terrified of Him.

Job 37:14: Listen to this, O Job, Stand and consider the wonders of God.

Psalm 8:3-5: When I consider Your heavens, the work of Your fingers, the moon and the stars, which You have ordained; What is man that You take thought of him, and the son of man that You care for him? Yet You have made him a little lower than God, and You crown him with glory and majesty!

Psalm 64:9: Then all men will fear, And they will declare the work of God, And will consider what He has done.

Psalm 107:43: Who is wise? Let him give heed to these things, and consider the lovingkindnesses of the LORD.

Ecclesiastes 7:13: Consider the work of God, For who is able to straighten what He has bent?

Luke 12:24-27: Consider the ravens, for they neither sow nor reap; they have no storeroom nor barn, and yet God feeds them; how much more valuable you are than the birds! And which of you by worrying can add a single hour to his life's span? If then you cannot do even a very little thing, why do you worry about other matters? Consider the lilies, how they grow: they neither toil nor spin; but I tell you, not even Solomon in all his glory clothed himself like one of these.

There is no one higher or greater than God. He is perfect in all His ways (Matt. 5:48) because He is sovereign. We do not understand the attributes of His nature through some outside or higher standard because His ways are the standard. By His nature we know holiness, grace, love, compassion, longsuffering, justice, and mercy. His ways are good because He is the Alpha and Omega, who was and is and is to come (Rev 1:8).

It is important to establish our understanding of the character of God so we can rightly speak of His will for the world and for our lives. In accordance with His perfect nature, God has provided a merciful way to justify us in spite of our sin. He is sovereign over creation, and because He loves us, He has established a just, fair, and impartial means for us to be saved. He has patiently waited for the fullness of time to pour out His wrath on the world so that by grace many may be saved through faith in Him. He shows no favoritism in His witness to the world through His creation and Spirit.

DOES THE BIBLE ALWAYS PRESENT GOD AS RECONIZIBLY GOOD?

There are several events recorded throughout the Scriptures which may lead us to question the goodness of God. And, I confess, at first reading some of what the Scriptures record about God's treatment of sinners does not seem to be so "recognizably good" from our vantage point. For example, many ask questions such as, "If God is good, why would He flood the earth and kill all those innocent babies?"

In events such as the flood, it should be noted that prior to bringing judgement on the land for the people's evil ways, God always provided a warning and a way of redemption for those who would simply repent and trust Him. God did provide an ark, called Noah to preach repentance (2 Peter 3:20), and even waited over one hundred years before the flood to allow the people time to change their minds. Therefore, a more appropriate question might be, "Why did the parents of those children refuse to believe and allow them to receive God's provision?"

Suppose the largest tsunami in human history is about to wipe out your entire town and you are the only one who knows it. You go around warning everyone and begging them to leave as soon as possible. If some of the families refuse to heed your warning, is it your fault if they and their children perish, or is it their fault? We must be careful not to blame God for the rebellion of

His creation, especially in light of His undeserved provisions and merciful patience.

We must also remember what kind of world it was at the time of the flood. Scripture says:

Genesis 6:5: Then the LORD saw that the wickedness of man was great on the earth, and that every intent of the thoughts of his heart was only evil continually.

In a world filled with rapes, child sacrifices, cannibalism and all types of gross evil that our sensitive Westernized minds cannot even begin to fathom, I suspect that a child's death would be better than to be raised by the likes of those who walked the earth at this time.

Many today consider death to be final and thus the worse kind of evil, but we as Christians do not believe this. For us death is a passage into an afterlife that, for children who have not reached a moral age of accountability, would be far better than the hell on earth in store for them if they had continued to live. In other words, death should not be seen as the worse option in these types of dire situations.

There is another principle here we should remember. We simply are not knowledgeable enough to fully comprehend all the ways of our Lord. As Scripture reminds us,

Deuteronomy 29:29: The secret things belong to the LORD our God, but the things revealed belong to us and to our children forever.

Those of us who have had the privilege of being parents have learned that there are often choices we have to make that impact our young children negatively which they simply may not be mature enough to understand. On some level we have to acknowledge the same principle must apply to God's choices in relation to His creation. C.S. Lewis addressed this profound truth in a book titled *The Problem of Pain* when he wrote,

> ...if God is wiser than we, His judgments must differ from ours on many things, and not least on good and evil. What seems to us good may therefore not be good in His eyes, and what seems to us evil may not be evil... That does not mean that what we consider good could be completely different from what God considers good. That would make it empty to speak of God as 'good' and it would take away all moral reasons for loving and obeying Him.[4]

While there are certainly some mysteries regarding how an infinite, all-knowing Creator interacts with His finite creation, the Scripture simply leaves no room for

---

[4] C.S. Lewis, *The Problem of Pain*, 16, 28-29. Lewis does not claim to solve the problem of evil. He instead warns his readers that we should not expect full understanding regarding God's ways with regard to evil and suffering. As finite creatures, we cannot understand how "the sufferings of this present time are not to be compared with the glory which shall be revealed in us" (Rom. 8:18).

mystery regarding the goodness of God. When it comes to sinful decisions and moral evil, it is fine to appeal to the mystery of man's capriciousness, but not of God's character. The goodness of God's character is not something our Scriptures leave a mystery.

Finally, it should also be noted that the Scriptures employ many various idioms, metaphors, metonymies, hyperboles, and other literary devices of which the common reader may simply be unfamiliar. For instance, God, especially in Old Testament writings, is often substituted as the blame or cause for things He merely permitted to occur, which is an example of a figure of speech called *metonymy*.[5]

For example, one may say, "The US President has put Iraq into shambles." While the sitting President's action of withdrawing the troops and remaining passive may have led to violent events done by bad characters in Iraq, obviously the President himself did not act to directly cause the violence in Iraq (nor did he likely desire this outcome). Likewise, sometimes biblical authors may attribute actions to God based on His passivity, not His active agency. James, the brother of Jesus, warns against drawing false conclusions by blaming God for moral evil:

---

[5] "Metonymy is a figure of speech in which an author uses a word (or words) for another word (or words) based upon either a sequential, spatial, temporal, or attributive association between the two." Carl D. DuBois, *Metonymy and Synecdoche in the New Testament*, (SIL International, 1999), 2.

James 1:13-15: When tempted, no one should say, "God is tempting me." For God cannot be tempted by evil, nor does he tempt anyone; but each person is tempted when they are dragged away by their own evil desire and enticed. Then, after desire has conceived, it gives birth to sin; and sin, when it is full-grown, gives birth to death.

Someone may wish to make a philosophical argument which goes something like this:

God knew for certain that I would be tempted and He did not stop it, thus He must have willed that I be tempted. And if so, He must also have known with certainty that I would sin when tempted, therefore God determined my sin.

Is this the philosophical answer that James concluded? No, quite the opposite in fact. He clearly and unequivocally removes God from any implication in the temptation or the resulting sin by putting the blame back onto "their own evil desire."

James, like Jesus before him, corrected many of the common misconceptions and false conclusions drawn by those who followed the Essenes' fatalistic teachings, which were well known around Nazareth and the surrounding area in that day.[6] This is why we must

---

[6] Some scholars argue that Joseph, Mary, Elizabeth, John the Baptist, James (the brother of Jesus), and those close to that family would have been most influenced by the Essenes, a branch of Pharisees which conformed to the most rigid rules of Levitical purity. Josephus wrote, "The doctrine of the Essenes tends to teach all men that they confidently

interpret all Scripture through the Word, who is the Christ, the complete and final revelation of God's character and what He wished to reveal to His creation.

Just as it would be unfair for you to pass judgement on the actions of a police officer, doctor, lawyer (or anyone whose decisions may impact the life of others) without being familiar with all the details of the case, so too it is unfair for anyone to judge God based on a short-sighted and ill-informed understanding of the full historical and literary context of each instance.

While it is not this book's aim to provide an apologetic defense of every troubling text, be assured that there is no shortage of material available for those who are willing to sincerely and objectively understand all the facts before passing rushed judgement on the character of our Maker.

---

may trust their fate in the hands of God, and nothing happens without his will." In his *Antiquities* (xiii. 5, § 9), Josephus speaks of the Essenes as a sect which had existed in the time of the Maccabees, contemporaneously with the Pharisees and Sadducees, and which teaches that all things are determined by destiny (εἱμαρμένη), and that nothing befalls men which has not been foreordained; whereas the Pharisees make allowance for free will, and the Sadducees deny destiny altogether. The Essenes are believed to have become a part of the Gnostic movement which lead to much controversy with the Early Church Fathers. Kaufmann Kohler, (*Jewish Encyclopedia*, 1906). Quotes take from: http://www.jewishencyclopedia.com/articles/5867-essenes [date accessed 12/14/18].

Chapter 1

What is the Gospel?

God's Provision is Good News

The news about God is good because God's character is good. If He was not a good God, then there would be no such thing as good news because there would be no motive for Him to provide salvation. The news brought to us through the Scripture is that our God is a loving Creator and Ruler who would rather show mercy than justice toward undeserving sinners. God has provided the means of salvation for all people, at all times, and in all places, not because He has to, but because He is good, and that truth is the very heart of what we call the gospel.

Mankind is not left to be slaves to what sin and death bring – judgment and wrath. Every single morally accountable person has, at some point, the opportunity to be reconciled to God.

Romans 10:12-13: For there is no distinction between Jew and Greek; for the same Lord is Lord of all, abounding in riches for all who call on Him; for "WHOEVER WILL CALL ON THE NAME OF THE LORD WILL BE SAVED."

The gospel is the truth that whoever calls upon the name of the Lord (by seeking Him in faith) will be saved (Ps. 145:18; Joel 2:32; Ps. 18:3; Zech. 13:9; Acts 2:21). Men have been obeying the gospel since the beginning, yes even before the cross (Gen. 4:26; Gen. 12:8; Ex. 34:5; Ps. 99:6). And the gospel has continued to be proclaimed and obeyed after the cross (Acts 2:21; Rom. 10:12-13; 1 Cor. 1:2).

HOW WERE PEOPLE SAVED PRIOR TO CHRIST'S COMING?

No one has ever been saved outside of the gospel, for "it is the power of God for salvation to all who believe" (Rom. 1:16-17). The gospel calls all to repent and trust in the Lord for salvation, and be forgiven and credited with righteousness so as to receive the gift of eternal life.

There has always been one gospel and it is the eternal gospel. Whoever repents and trusts in the Lord for their salvation and calls upon His name in faith is forgiven and credited with righteousness, being set apart in the Son. They are set apart, being in Christ, based on His work on the cross, who came down to earth as a man and atoned for the sins of all people.

Salvation comes by hearing and trusting the gospel, the news of God's goodness and provision. This has been the good news since Adam and Eve left the garden. It has never changed; it has only been more fully revealed. By grace through faith, mankind is credited with righteousness and saved. They are placed in Christ (His work on the cross) and are baptized into Him. They abide in Him and produce His fruit. They are part of His body. They are marked with the Holy Spirit who will resurrect them to eternal life.

THE UNIVERSAL WITNESS

God has personally made known the gospel (the "good news") to all creatures under heaven since the very beginning of time. The Lord has sown the knowledge of Himself and the call of the gospel into the hearts of all people, making His appeal for their reconciliation. He has made known the good news to everyone through His creation.

Obviously, people are not born knowing about Jesus in specific, or about His death, burial, and resurrection. But, specific knowledge of Jesus and His work on the cross is not all that the gospel entails. Christ's work is both the foundation and fulfillment of the "gospel," which is the "good news" that has been made known from the very beginning.

The good news is that God is gracious to save whoever repents of their wrong doing and places their trust in Him. By faith anyone may be forgiven and credited as righteous (Heb. 11; Rom. 4:22-24). All may be saved by God's grace because He is free to show mercy to whomever He pleases (Rom. 9:15). This truth has been a reality from the beginning of creation, not just since the first century.

The Old Testament saints were saved through the gospel, and they had no specific knowledge of Jesus and his death, burial or resurrection. This was a part of "the mystery of Christ" that had been hidden for generations (1 Cor. 2:7; Eph. 3:3-5). They knew God was the only one that could save them from their sin, but they did not know how He was going to do it while maintaining His justice. Jesus and His work on the cross was a "shadow" and a "mystery" that had not yet been fully revealed (Rom. 16:25-26).

What the Old Testament saints did not realize was that the God they knew was none other than the Lord and Savior, Jesus Christ. Christ was (and still is) the "I Am" (John 8:58) that freed them from Egypt. Christ was the One that spoke to them, and gave them the gospel, and the One in whom they put their faith. No one has seen or heard from the Father except the Son (John 1:18; 5:37; 6:46). The Son is the complete and authoritative revelation of God to this world. In other words, everything we know about God must be filtered through what has been revealed through Jesus.

Jesus taught us that the gospel has always been the same, in both the Old Testament and the New Testament. God gave His word that sin leads to death. God gave His word that He would provide a way for salvation. God gave His word that He will forgive mankind for their sins and credit them with righteousness. How can God do all this? Through His Son, Jesus, the Word!

Since the coming of Christ, mankind obviously understands more fully how the gospel is accomplished. After all, the mystery has now been revealed that God the Son came in the flesh, died on the cross providing atonement for all sins, and was raised on the third day.

Christ not only shows God's righteousness in passing over sins previously committed (Rom. 3:25; 2 Cor. 5:19), but His sacrifice satisfies the justice of God by providing a payment for all sin (Rom. 3:26). By applying the Son's atonement to all who believe, God is able to overcome death which sin naturally produces. Those who do not trust in God and His promise do not receive Christ's atonement, and will suffer the just penalty due to their rebellion.

Christ's life, death, and resurrection are the definitive testimony and fulfillment of the gospel, for God desires all mankind to be saved (1 Tim. 2:4). God takes no delight in the death of the wicked (Ez. 18:23). God is patient towards all, because He does not wish for anyone to perish (2 Peter 3:9). God is perfectly fair, just and impartially sovereign over the universe (Rom. 2:11; Acts 10:34; Eph. 6:9; James 2:1; 8-9).

God's righteous and loving character can be seen in His plan and purpose for mankind. He is sovereign over creation, and does not need mankind to give testimony of His good news, though He does graciously call and allow people to serve this noble purpose. Because He loves all people, and because He is impartial, He shows no favoritism in the witness of the gospel to the entire world (Rom. 2:11).

We can know God is good–*recognizably* good. Through instilling his law in our hearts, the natural revelation of the goodness of creation, and God's universal provision of the gospel to all mankind in all times, God has revealed His absolute goodness to every man, woman, boy and girl.

Chapter 2

What About Those Who Have Never Heard?

God's Provision is Universal

The inquiry posed by the title of this chapter is one of the most asked questions among Christians today. But the question itself has a faulty premise. Should we assume that not everyone has seen, heard and understood enough about God to respond positively to His revelation?

The apostle Paul certainly did not think so. The unreached people groups of his day were simply referred to as "the Gentiles" because up to that point the special (or *specific*) revelation of the law and the prophets had typically been reserved for the Jews.

What does Paul conclude about the uninformed Gentile people who had never heard the words of Abraham, Moses, or the prophets of the Old Testament? He said that they all are "without excuse" (Rom. 1:20) because the news about God has been sufficiently made clear by other, more natural means, such as creation and their conscience.

In Romans 1:16-2:16 for instance, the apostle Paul declares that the powerful gospel appeal has been sent first to the Jew and then the Gentile (1:16) and "the righteous will live by faith" (1:17). The Psalmist put it this way:

Psalm 19:1-8: The heavens are telling of the glory of God; And their expanse is declaring the work of His hands. Day to day pours forth speech, And night to night reveals knowledge. There is no speech, nor are there words; Their voice is not heard. Their line has gone out through all the earth, And their utterances to the end of the world. In them He has placed a tent for the sun, Which is as a bridegroom coming out of his chamber; It rejoices as a strong man to run his course. Its rising is from one end of the heavens, And its circuit to the other end of them; And there is nothing hidden from its heat. The law of the LORD is perfect, restoring the soul; The testimony of the LORD is sure, making wise the simple. The precepts of the LORD are right, rejoicing the heart; The commandment of the LORD is pure, enlightening the eyes.

Paul, in Romans 1, then goes on to explain that those who continue "to suppress the truth in unrighteousness" will be given over to their defiled minds and cut off from further light of God's gracious truth (1:24-26). In other words, those who continually suppress clearly revealed truth, whether Jew or Gentile, by "trading it in for lies" will grow more and more calloused. Eventually, their consciences will become seared (1 Tim. 4:2), their hearts hardened (John 12:40), and they may no longer be morally capable to see, hear, understand and turn to God for healing (Acts 28:23-28) without something significant provoking their wills (Rom. 11:14).

On the other hand, if one acknowledges the truth revealed about God through general or specific means of revelation, He is faithful to bring them more light. Those who are faithful with a little will be given more (Matt. 13:12; Acts 17:27; John 6:45).

In other words, Paul concludes that both the specific light of revelation sent to Israel through the Scriptures and the natural light of God's revelation brought through creation and conscience is sufficient to lead anyone and everyone to faith in Him. For this reason, no one has any excuse for their unbelief.

Since everyone has a sufficient amount of light to see and believe in Him so as to receive more light, no one has any excuse for failing to acknowledge God as their God. As Paul explained it:

Romans 1:20: For since the creation of the world God's invisible qualities—his eternal power and divine nature—have been clearly seen, being understood from what has been made, so that people are without excuse.

Those who respond in faith to the general light of God's common revelation will be entrusted with the full light of Christ.

Matthew 13:12: Whoever has will be given more, and they will have an abundance. Whoever does not have, even what they have will be taken from them.

Luke 16:10: He who is faithful in a very little thing is faithful also in much…

Titus 2:11: For the grace of God has appeared that offers salvation to all people.

John 1:9: The true light that gives light to everyone was coming into the world.

In the following chapters, we will discuss the purpose of divine revelation and the plight of those who never hear the specific truth about Jesus.

Chapter 3

What is Special about Revelation?

God's Provision has Purpose

When it comes to revelation, scholars speak in terms of two distinct kinds: God's general and special revelation. General revelation is just that, God making Himself known generally through the natural world and moral conscience. Special revelation consists of His Word, the Messiah and His inspired message, preserved for us in the Scriptures.

These terms can be unclear, however. Calling some aspects of God's revelation "special" may give the impression that it is more effective in accomplishing its purpose than the rest of God's clearly revealed truth. But God's purposes never fail. If He sends revelation to accomplish a given purpose, it will accomplish that purpose. So, instead of "special revelation" we prefer the term "specific revelation" because that better connotes its proper meaning. God is making known the specifics in accomplishing redemption for the world.

IS REVELATION SUFFICIENT TO SAVE?

At this point some tend to ask if the general revelation through natural means is sufficient to save. No, but neither is the specific revelation of the Scripture. Only the grace of God through the payment of Christ's blood can save anyone, regardless of how they respond to any means of divine revelation.

Paul is putting all revelation on the same level by showing that whether one is a Jew, who has read all the prophets, or one is a Gentile, who has never heard these scriptural teachings, does not matter because all revelation is sufficient to accomplish what the Bible says it was meant to accomplish.

General revelation was sent so that all may acknowledge God as God (Rom. 1:20-21; Rev. 14:6-7), whereas specific (or *special*) revelation was sent so that all may believe in Christ for eternal life (John 20:31). The light of revelation is sent so all may see, know and understand truth. It is mankind's responsibility to acknowledge and put their trust in that truth, which all people are morally able (and thus responsible) to do until they have physically died—or possibly grown so calloused and blinded by their own rebellion that God judicially cuts them off from further light.[7]

---

[7] Even the Jews who were cut off for their unbelief (Rom. 11:20) were able to be grafted back in if they left their unbelief (Rom. 11:23), so no one should conclude that God's judicial act of cutting one off is retributive or final, but instead should be understood as merciful and hopeful (Rom. 11:32). Even Paul believed his own ministry may provoke their hard hearts to envy so that they too may be saved (Rom. 11:14).

No one is saved by revelation. We are saved by grace through faith which comes by the means of divine revelation, God's word (Rom 10:17-18). God's self-revelation is purely gracious. He does not owe us anything. His work to reveal Himself is the gracious provision that is at the heart of the gospel itself. God is faithful to draw near to all who acknowledge Him as God through the light they have been given (Acts 17:27; John 6:45; Matt. 13:12).

In a 1981 sermon on Romans 2, Pastor John MacArthur seemed to affirm this view when he said:

> Creation, conduct, conscience, contemplation, what they do, how they deal with the good and bad in their own life and how they deal with it in the lives of others indicates that they know the law of God as written in them. Now, here is the most important thing I've said yet. The sum of it is this: If they live up to that much light, and they accept that much light, God will reveal to them the full light of Jesus Christ. I believe that with all my heart. You see, that's what it says in Acts 17, 'He is not far from us if we would feel after Him.' You see? If they would just take what they have and accept that. John 7:17 — mark it down. 'If any man wills to do My Father's

Will, he shall know of the teaching.' If the willing heart is there, he'll know.[8]

WHAT ABOUT THOSE WHO HAVE NEVER HEARD ABOUT JESUS SPECIFICALLY?

If Jesus is the only way for salvation, then what does that mean for those who have never heard about Him specifically? It is one thing to hear and reject the good news about Jesus, but to be condemned for rejecting a message you never heard just does not seem fair.

There is just one problem with that reasoning. Sinners are primarily condemned for their sin, not for rejecting the grace that covers their sin. Our sin is an offense against an eternally holy God, thus the only just punishment will have an everlasting effect, which the Scripture describes in horrific terms as a place called hell (Matt. 25:31-46).

Granted, only those who reject God's gracious provision will be judged for their sin, but that does not mean their initial condemnation is based upon that rejection. Because all have sinned (Rom. 3:23) and sinners are ultimately under condemnation for sin, no one can rightly claim they fell under condemnation

---

[8] MacArthur has since clarified his position as not affirming that the light of general revelation is sufficient to lead fallen humanity to genuine faith in God. This, in our opinion, gives back the very excuse Paul was intending to remove in Romans 1:20, and appears to undermine the point of divine impartiality in judgment that MacArthur was attempting to establish in that original 1981 sermon.

because of how they replied to the specific news about Jesus.

So, people may remain under condemnation for their sin because they reject the provisions being offered to them by God, but they are not initially put under condemnation based on their responses to these offers. They are condemned for their own willful sin against a Holy God and they remain under that condemnation until they receive His gracious provision.

Justice demands punishment for all who sin against God. The good news is that God has made a way for all to be rescued from this just punishment through trusting in Him. God does not owe salvation, or even the means to be saved, to anyone. Therefore, it is wrong-minded to approach this question as if any sinner deserves more than divine justice.

The good news is that our heavenly Father desires mercy over justice (James 2:13; Matt. 5:38-48; 12:7). He is a loving and gracious God who does not want any to perish but all to come to repentance (2 Peter 3:9; 1 Tim. 2:4; Ezk. 18:30-32). God is all-loving and perfect in every way, so we can trust that He will always do what is good, even when we do not understand. While Scripture may not give us perfect clarity on this topic, we do have some strong biblical insight that helps guide our thinking, which will be unpacked further in the coming chapters.

41

Chapter 4

Are God And His Ways Knowable?

God's Provision is Clear

Gd's eternal power, divine nature and invisible qualities, is plain for everyone to see and understand. As mentioned earlier, this is referred to as God's "general revelation," which renders all people "without excuse" for their unbelief (Rom. 1:19-20; Acts 14:17; Heb. 3:4; Ps. 19:1). While this revelation is not sufficient to lead one to specific faith in Jesus, there is strong biblical evidence to support that it is sufficient to lead one to acknowledge and fear God, which subsequently leads to further revelation (Luke 16:10-12).

J.I. Packer, a notable biblical scholar, taught "that God's general revelation, even when correctly grasped, yields knowledge of creation, providence, and judgment only, not of grace that restores sinners to fellowship with

God."[9] While this is certainly true, nothing in the text suggests that mankind is not freely able to respond to such revelation by either "exchanging the truth for lies" (Rom. 1:25) or "retaining the knowledge of God" (Rom. 1:28). An innate moral inability to respond to this revelation would nullify the point of the apostle in declaring that all are "without excuse" (i.e., "I was born morally unable to respond positively to God's revelation.").

THE PROBLEM OF SIN REMAINS

This ability to respond (responsibility) in light of God's clear revelation does not solve the problem of sin and the need for redemption, however. Even those who acknowledge God as God still deserve condemnation for their sin (just as Abel still needed atonement as referenced in our first chapter).

Sinners who respond in reverent fear and attempt to be faithful to His laws (or their conscience) are still sinners. They still deserve hell and condemnation because they will always fall short of all the law demands (Rom. 3:10-11, 23). Even their good deeds would be as worthless as filthy rags given the penalty due for their sin (Isa. 64:6).

---

[9] J.I. Packer, "Are Non-Christian Faiths Ways of Salvation?" *Bibliotheca Sacra*, BSAC 130:518 (Apr 1973). Quote taken from: http://www.galaxie.com/article/bsac130-518-02 [date accessed 9/11/17].

Abraham, long before Jesus came, genuinely believed in God and it was credited to him as righteousness (Gen. 15:6; Rom. 4:3), yet Abraham still needed a Savior to atone for his sin. Cornelius, prior to hearing the good news of Jesus, was a worshipper who feared the Lord and was shown favor (Acts 10), but his sin debt remained.

Throughout the Scriptures we see examples of God "finding favor" in believing individuals (Job, Enoch, Noah, Abram, Rahab, etc.), but these people, like all of humanity, still fell short of God's glory and were unrighteous according to the demands of God's law (Rom. 3:10-23). They needed a Savior. They needed redemption and reconciliation.

Even those who believe the truth of God's revelation deserve eternal punishment for their sin. This is why no one can claim to have merited or earned their salvation by placing their faith in God. If faith alone was sufficient to merit salvation, there would have been no need for the cross. Jesus atones for the sins of the world so that whoever believes in Him may be shown mercy by a gracious and righteous God, a God who is demonstrably good.

What must be understood is that no one is righteous according to the demands of the law. However, that does not mean that all people are morally unable to believe God's revealed truth so as to be credited as righteous by God's grace.

Paul taught that no one was righteous in Romans 3, yet he turns around and declares in the very next chapter that "Abraham believed God, and it was credited to him as righteousness" (4:3). How can that be? Has Paul contradicted himself? First, he declares that no one is righteous and then he tells us that Abraham was righteous? Which is it?

Paul is drawing the distinction between righteousness by law through works (Rom. 3:10-11) and righteousness by grace through faith (Rom. 3:21-24; 27-28). The former is unattainable, but the latter has always been very much attainable by anyone, which again, is why all are "without excuse" for unbelief in God's abundantly clear revelation (Rom. 1:20).

CORRECTING A FALSE ASSUMPTION

Some theologians teach that all of humanity are born "God haters" due to their fallen condition and can do nothing except reject the good news brought by the Spirit because of their innate animosity toward their Creator. According to this theological perspective, God's own appeals for reconciliation are insufficient to enable a fallen person to respond freely. For instance, the current President of Southern Baptist Theological Seminary, Albert Mohler, gave his exposition on Romans 1:18-32:

"Paul's story of universal human sinfulness and depravity is our story. In these words, we discover the explanation of how it is that we find ourselves in this condition of sinfulness... Every single human being is part of the intellectual activity described here. All descendants of Adam are involved in the suppression of 'truth in unrighteousness'... This text is about humanity. The verb tense in the phrase 'God gave' is past tense — this has *already* happened. God has given humanity over. The apostle Paul includes everyone in the indictment as he describes the giving over of all of humanity to sinfulness"... Theologically, this is referred to as the noetic consequences of the fall. The phrase 'noetic effects' refers to the intellectual consequences of sin..."[10]

Mohler continues in this message to expound upon a doctrine called "Total Inability," the belief that all of humanity is born morally incapable of responding positively to any appeal of God unless they are first regenerated by an "irresistible" or "effectual" work of grace.

In other words, Mohler believes people must be born again (regenerated) before they can believe in God's own appeals to be reconciled through faith in Christ (i.e., pre-faith regeneration). Mohler seems convinced that God's gracious work in sending His Son,

---

[10] Albert Mohler, "The Way the World Thinks: Meeting the Natural Mind in the Mirror and in the Marketplace" (Desiring God National Conference, 2010). Quote taken from: https://www.desiringgod.org/messages/the-way-the-world-thinks-meeting-the-natural-mind-in-the-mirror-and-in-the-marketplace [date accessed: 12/2/2017].

the Spirit, the Apostles, the Scripture, His Bride and the gospel appeal needs yet another gracious work (a prior "irresistible work") to be sufficient to enable a positive response.

Does God's gracious work really need more grace to work? And must God's gracious gifts be irresistibly applied for Him to get full credit for giving them? I do not believe so.

What Mohler apparently fails to recognize is that Paul is contrasting "the righteous who live by faith" in Rom. 1:17 with those who "suppress the truth in unrighteousness" in verse 18.

Paul is not attempting to say that every human has continually suppressed the truth in unrighteousness, traded the truth in for lies, been given over to their defiled minds, become homosexuals and approve of all who do these sinful acts. Paul is attempting to demonstrate how all people (both the Jews with the direct revelation of God's law and the Gentiles with only their inborn conscience) have broken the commandments of God and thus may only attain righteous by grace through faith in God—not by meritorious works of the law.

Here is a key point! Proof that no one is morally capable of attaining righteousness by works of the law is not proof that no one is morally capable of believing in God so as to be credited as righteous by His gracious provision through Christ. Read that last sentence again until it really sinks in, because it is key in understanding Paul's overall point in the first three chapters of Romans. It is also vital to understanding the goodness of God's provision for all people!

Chapter 5

Are Fallen Men Responsible To God's Revelation?

God's Provision is Receivable

Fallen people can respond willingly to God's gracious appeals to be reconciled from that fallen condition. We must understand that there is a difference in being culpable for sinful immorality and growing calloused to divine revelation sent to rescue us from our sinful condition. The former does not necessarily imply the latter. This is why we can affirm the concept of "original sin" (man is born with sinful inclinations and in need of a Savior) while seeing men as maintaining their moral ability to respond (responsibility) to God's revelation.

This distinction speaks to the natural man's abilities to respond to the light of God's revelation in contrast to their culpability for sin. When one confounds these two doctrines it becomes as difficult as untangling a wad of fishing line to correct. One cannot assume culpability for sin equals a moral inability to recognize and confess one's sin in light of God's revealed truth.

51

Is there any Biblical reason to suggest that man is not "able-to-respond" for that which God holds him "response-able?" Paul's declaration of no one having any excuses for unbelief in light of God's clear revelation (Rom. 1:20) certainly suggests no good excuse exists. Paul teaches that men's "thinking became futile and their foolish hearts were darkened…therefore God gave them over in the sinful desires" (vs. 21, 24). They were not born futile, darkened and given over due to the fall. Paul is revealing the natural result of those who continue to ignore God's revelation and "trade the truth in for lies." Not everyone who has ever lived would match the description of the apostle in Romans 1:18-32. After all, he is contrasting those who suppress truth in unrighteousness with "the righteous who live by faith" referenced earlier in verse 17. Some people feared the Lord, worshipped Him in earnest and believed in the revelation they received (Heb. 11). They did not trade the truth of God in for lies and become hardened to the revelation of God due to their consistent rebellion.

In Romans 1:1-3:20, Paul is attempting to demonstrate that both Jews and Gentiles have fallen short of the demands of God's law. He is not attempting to teach that man is born morally unable to respond in faith to the revelation of God. That would give them back the very excuse he took away in verse 20 of the first chapter.

The reason this has become such a perplexing question for so many students of the Bible is because some have confounded Paul's teaching to suggest that man is morally unable to acknowledge God in light of His general revelation and yet we are to believe He holds mankind "responsible" for their reply to that revelation. This confounds even the most discerning believer because it appears to be anything but just.

Are we to believe that a good God would send a light that is bright enough to condemn all people, but yet too dim for any lost person to actually respond in faith to it? More significantly, are God's appeals for the lost to be reconciled from their fallen condition insufficient to enable a fallen person to respond willingly to those appeals?

It is one thing for parents to discipline their children for a misdeed by grounding them to their room. It is a whole other thing for parents to lock the door from the outside and then hold the children responsible for not coming out when called. Likewise, it is possible for us to affirm mankind's complete culpability for sin (i.e., being sent to their room) while still rejecting the notion that God has disabled sinners from responding to His own appeals to be reconciled (i.e., locking the door so as to disable one from responding positively to appeals for reconciliation).[11]

Everyone has what they need to respond to God. No one anywhere in this world has any excuse for his or her unbelief. Mankind is responsible to all of God's revelation because they are "able-to-respond" to all of God's revelation. If they acknowledge the truth of the little revelation that they have received, then God is faithful to entrust them with more (Matt. 25:21). If they trade the truth in for lies, then they have no excuse (Rom. 1:20; Rev. 14:7-8; Acts 10:34-35).

In short, general revelation is sufficient to lead anyone to know God's specific (or *special*) revelation, thus no one has any excuse for their unbelief.

CAN ANYONE SEEK GOD?

Paul taught, "...there is no one who understands; there is no one who seeks God" (Rom. 3:11). And to further demonstrate that all people have fallen short of the glory of God and broken His law, Paul quotes from the Psalmist, saying:

---

[11] Some have critiqued this analogy by pointing out the difference between a moral and physical inability (i.e. *it's not that they cannot come out, it's that they are not willing to come out*). This distinction is understood and addressed elsewhere, but this is an analogy meant to compare a physical inability to a moral one so as to demonstrate a point. That point is that the child is unable to come out for reasons beyond his control, which is true whether or not the innate inability is physical or moral.

Psalm 14:2-3: The Lord looks down from heaven on all mankind to see if there are any who understand, any who seek God. All have turned away, all have become corrupt; there is no one who does good, not even one.

Apart from God's gracious initiative in bringing His Son, the Holy Spirit, and the inspired gospel appeal, no one can merit salvation or consistently seek to obey God in a way that will attain their own righteousness by merit. In Romans chapter 3:10-20 the apostle is seeking to prove that no one can earn righteousness by means of the law. But in verse 21 he shifts to reveal a righteousness now "being made known" that can be obtained by means of grace through faith in Christ as opposed to merit. Being unable to attain righteousness by means of the law does not mean we are unable to obtain righteousness by means of grace through faith in Christ.

Of course, we all can affirm that no one is righteous with regard to the demands of the law. But there have been many throughout the pages of Scripture who have been declared righteous by means of grace through faith. We should not wrongly assume that because mankind is unable to fully keep the demands of the law that they are equally unable to admit their inability to keep those demands and trust in the One who has.

Proof that mankind is morally incapable of earning their own righteousness by doing meritorious works is not proof that mankind is morally incapable of believing and trusting in the righteousness of another. It must also be understood that placing one's trust in the righteousness of Christ is not earning one's own righteousness. Those who trust in Christ are graciously imputed with His righteousness, they are not earning or meriting their own.

Notice, if we go back to examine the context of Paul's original quote in Psalm 14, we read that he is specifically speaking of "the fool" who says, "there is no God," and then he contrasts between the "evil doers" and "His people...the generation of the righteous."

Psalm 14:1; 4-5: The fool says in his heart, "There is no God." They are corrupt, their deeds are vile; there is none who does good... Do all these evildoers know nothing? They devour my people as though eating bread; they never call on the LORD. But there they are overwhelmed with dread, for God is present in the company of the righteous.

There is no reason to presume that "the fool" who says "there is no God" does so inevitably because of an inborn nature resulting from the fall. Nor are there any grounds for attempting to make the case that "the generation of the righteous" who are considered "His people" were made so by some kind of effectual working of God. This text seems to clearly indicate that these "fools" trade the truth of God in for lies by freely denying His existence, though they could and should have chosen otherwise. Those who become "His" do so by grace through a free response of faith.

One cannot merely assume that fallen man is born morally incapable of responding in faith to God's inspired and powerful appeal to be reconciled from that fall. To establish this biblically one must demonstrate how our fallen condition prevents us from responding willingly. Additionally, it would need to be explained why a just God would seal mankind in a fallen/disabled condition from birth and still hold them responsible for their rejection of His own genuine appeals, even though they have no control over their naturally disabled condition and subsequent "choices" to reject God's genuine offer of forgiveness.

Romans 3:11 seems to fit nicely with other teachings of Scripture about man's responsibility to seek God, such as:

Acts 17:26-27: From one man he made all the nations, that they should inhabit the whole earth; and he marked out their appointed times in history and the boundaries of their lands. God did this so that they would seek him and perhaps reach out to him and find him, though he is not far from any one of us.

Isaiah 55:6-7: Seek the LORD while He may be found; call upon Him while He is near. Let the wicked forsake his way And the unrighteous man his thoughts; And let him return to the LORD, And He will have compassion on him, And to our God, for He will abundantly pardon.

Zephaniah 2:3: Seek the LORD, all you humble of the land, you who do what he commands. Seek righteousness, seek humility; perhaps you will be sheltered on the day of the LORD'S anger.

2 Chronicles 12:14: He did evil because he did not set his heart to seek the LORD.

Psalms 83:16: Fill their faces with dishonor, That they may seek Your name, O LORD.

2 Chronicles 20:3: Jehoshaphat was afraid and turned his attention to seek the LORD, and proclaimed a fast throughout all Judah.

Luke 12:30-31: For all these things the nations of the world eagerly seek; but your Father knows that you need these things. But seek His kingdom, and these things will be added to you.

Chapter 6

Can Everyone Believe The Gospel?

God's Provision is Sufficient

What is the natural ability of man to respond willingly to God? Christian theists do not believe in mother nature, so to say that something is "natural" is to say that is it designed (or at least permitted) by God within His created order. From the beginning, we see that mankind could *naturally* hear the voice of God and respond with a humble confession.

Genesis 3:8-10: They heard the sound of the LORD God walking in the garden in the cool of the day, and the man and his wife hid themselves from the presence of the LORD God among the trees of the garden. Then the LORD God called to the man, and said to him, "Where are you?" He said, "I heard the sound of You in the garden, and I was afraid because I was naked; so I hid myself."

God called to Adam and he responded by confessing his fear. Are we to assume this vulnerable reply was actually brought about by some type of inner effectual work of divine grace, or was Adam simply responding freely to the loving call of a God genuinely seeking him in his brokenness?

During the curses that follow the fall, we do not see God punishing mankind by making them unable to respond willingly to His own revelation. When God was explaining the curse of labor pains and toiling the soil, did He forget to mention the worst of all the curses, "You now are morally incapable of responding willingly to my appeals for reconciliation?"

The story of Cain and Abel also illustrates this natural responsibility:

Genesis 4:3-7: So it came about in the course of time that Cain brought an offering to the LORD of the fruit of the ground. Abel, on his part also brought of the firstlings of his flock and of their fat portions. And the LORD had regard for Abel and for his offering; but for Cain and for his offering He had no regard. So Cain became very angry and his countenance fell. Then the LORD said to Cain, "Why are you angry? And why has your countenance fallen? If you do well, will not your countenance be lifted up? And if you do not do well, sin is crouching at the door; and its desire is for you, but you must master it."

The Lord clearly expresses an expectation for Cain to "do well" like his brother. This "well doing" was in reference to the offering (trusting the Lord), not meritorious works (deeds in attempt to earn salvation). The only hope for Cain "to master the sin crouching at his door" is to trust in the provision of his God (demonstrated in the offering), which he is clearly expected to do and which his brother did do.

There is no biblical indication that mankind lost their moral ability to respond willingly to God's own gracious provision due to the fall. What fallen humanity cannot do, now that they have been cast out of the garden and removed from their intimate fellowship with God, is understand deep spiritual mysteries hidden in the mind of God. The only way they can come to understand these truths is if God graciously sends them clear revelation, like He does by inspiring apostles and prophets to explain the purpose of the law in pointing us to the gospel (Rom. 10:14; Eph. 3:1-11).

IS THE GOSPEL A MYSTERY?

A "mystery" is a secret; something that is not fully revealed or able to be understood. The Bible often speaks of "the mystery of the gospel." Does this mean the gospel truth is not understandable? Does this mean that the gospel cannot be accepted and believed? Let's look at a passage where "mystery" is used in reference to the gospel:

Romans 16:25-27: Now to Him who is able to establish you according to my gospel and the preaching of Jesus Christ, according to the revelation

61

of the mystery which has been kept secret for long ages past, but now is manifested, and by the Scriptures of the prophets, according to the commandment of the eternal God, has been made known to all the nations, leading to obedience of faith; to the only wise God, through Jesus Christ, be the glory forever. Amen.

The specific truth claims of the gospel (salvation is provided by means of atonement through Christ's death and resurrection) were a mystery before they were made known through the divine inspiration of Scripture. These truths are no longer a mystery or a secret being hidden in riddles, or behind a veil, or a spirit of stupor (Mark 4; Matt. 13; 1 Cor. 2:7-8; Eph. 3:1-8; Rom 11:7). The riddle has been solved, the veil has been torn, and the spirit of stupor has been replaced with the Holy Spirit sent to bring conviction and clarity to the world!

These glorious truths were once hidden for a good redemptive purpose, but now they are clear for anyone and everyone to know and accept. No one can say, "I could not understand the truth of the gospel due to some innate moral inability beyond my control." We each will be judged by the very words of Christ (John 12:48) because they are clear, understandable and able to be accepted or suppressed.

If you suppress the truth you will eventually grow calloused to it (Rom. 1:18-32; Heb. 3:7-8; Acts 28:27-28), but no one is born morally incapable of seeing, hearing, understanding and turning to God for healing in response to the gospel revelation. The Scripture is the means God chose to make otherwise mysterious truths fully known. These deep mysteries were once hidden in the mind of God and not attainable by mankind, but praise be to God that He gave the apostles discernment by inspiring them to proclaim these deep truths clearly for all to know and accept them (1 Cor. 2:6-14; Eph. 3:1-8).

Chapter 7

Does God's Grace Need More Grace To Work?

God's Provision is Gracious

I f my wife gives me a list of things to get at the grocery store, then that list enables me to understand my wife's desire. Because of this, I may freely respond to her request by picking up those items from the store. Similarly, reading a powerful poem is sufficient to enable an emotional or thoughtful response within me. These are examples of common experiences of even those outside the church in everyday life.

Should we assume it is true that the natural man is able to freely respond in such a manner to the average grocery list or poem but not "God-breathed" revelation, unless graced in some additional supernatural manner? I see no biblical reason to come to this conclusion. Is God's own chosen means of revelation so insufficiently gracious that it needs an extra measure of grace to work?

God's gracious words need not a magical working (i.e., infused with some supernatural inner grace) to have their intended effect. They simply must be clear and understandable. The supernaturally inspired words of the gospel are sufficient to accomplish their biblically stated purpose without an additional supernatural working. Mankind has been created by God with the basic capacity to hear, understand and respond to clearly revealed truth. Those who do respond negatively to the clearly revealed truth of the gospel are not somehow morally restricted from doing otherwise. The natural man who deems the things of the Spirit foolish do so by their own free moral choice, not by an innate necessity which is beyond their control.

We commonly think of all humanity as born able to accept as true all the books offered up by the false religions of the world. People often put their trust in the lies offered by other worldviews, and even affirm them as being divinely authored. Are the claims of Christianity less able to be believed and affirmed as divinely inspired? Why should we accept the far-fetched claim that mankind is born able to place their trust in the claims of the Qur'an but not the Bible?

Why do so many seem to presume the Holy Spirit's inspired truth, preserved in the Scriptures and carried by the Holy Spirit-led Bride of Christ is not sufficient to enable the lost to respond willingly to it's appeals?

Does it make much sense to teach that mankind is born in a kind of fallen condition that makes them unable to even respond willingly to God's own powerful and gracious appeals to be reconciled from that fallen condition? Where does this presumption originate and why do so many today seem to accept it without question?

First, it should be noted that this assumption has not always been prevalent in the church:

Irenaeus, (130-202): "We have known the method of our salvation by no other means than those by whom the gospel came to us; which gospel they truly preached; but afterward, by the will of God, they delivered to us in the Scriptures, to be for the future the foundation and pillar of our faith." (Adv. H. 3:1)

Athanasius, (296-373): "The Holy Scriptures, given by inspiration of God, are of themselves sufficient toward the discovery of truth."

And, most importantly, we must examine the Scripture!

WHAT DOES THE BIBLE SAY ABOUT ITSELF?

There are many passages of Scripture that speak directly to the power and sufficiency of God's inspired word (John 20:31; Heb. 4:12; Rom. 10:17; 2 Tim. 3:16; Acts 20:32; 1 Peter 1:23; Isa. 55:11; Ps. 19:7-8; Heb. 1:1; John 6:63), but the most often referenced passage, in my experience, is...

Romans 1:16: For I am not ashamed of the gospel, for it is the power of God for salvation to everyone who believes, to the Jew first and also to the Greek.

N.T. Wright, a leading New Testament scholar, comments on this passage saying,

> This brief discussion of Paul's gospel thus indicates that, for him, 'the gospel', also translatable as 'the good news', was the power of the creator God. It is tempting to say, 'the gospel carried this divine power,' or 'the gospel conveyed this power.' Paul simply says it is this power.[12]

This is likely why Paul said with confidence to Timothy,

> **2 Timothy 3:15-16:** You have known the Holy Scriptures, which are able to make you wise for salvation through faith in Christ Jesus. All Scripture is God-breathed and is useful for teaching, rebuking, correcting and training in righteousness.

Is the nature of this divine revelation, God's inspired word, and all that God has done to reveal Himself to humanity, sufficient to enable a fallen man to respond willingly to His appeals? Focusing only on the nature of mankind ignores this question. Is the word of God, that which brought everything into existence, sufficiently powerful to accomplish the purpose for which the Scripture says it was sent?

> **Isaiah 55:11:** So will My word be which goes forth from My mouth; It will not return to Me empty,

---

[12] N.T. Wright, *Paul and the Faithfulness of God* (Minneapolis: Fortress, 2013), 916.

Without accomplishing what I desire, And without succeeding in the matter for which I sent it.

All Christians would have to admit that God's word is sufficient to accomplish its biblically stated purpose, but what is that purpose? Why did God have these powerful truths recorded for us and spread throughout the world? Let's allow the apostle John to answer that question for us:

John 20:31: These are written that you may believe that Jesus is the Messiah, the Son of God, and that by believing you may have life in his name.

The purpose for these truths being inspired and written is so "that you may believe," and the world along with you (John 17:21). So, do you think that God's purpose in having these inspired truths written have returned to Him void? I do not. The nature of the gospel and God's revelation is sufficient to enable a lost man to respond willingly to its appeals or instructions. There is no extra work God must do to change the nature of lost humanity to give the gospel a measure of sufficiency. In other words, God does not need to "reconcile" (fix) the nature of the fallen man in order to enable him to respond willingly to His own appeal to be reconciled from that fallen condition. This most certainly is putting the proverbial cart before the horse.

Chapter 8

Does The Bible Teach That The Gospel Is Not Able To Be Understood?

God's Provision is Understandable

Some theologians insist that 1 Corinthians 1:18-2:16 teaches that all lost people are morally incapable of understanding and accepting the gospel appeal, but is that really the intention of the apostle Paul? Let's unpack this passage more fully.

In this letter to the church of Corinth, a Greek port city, Paul uses a form of the word "wisdom" twenty-six times in just the first three chapters. Therefore, it is difficult to fully understand Paul's intention without first having a firm grasp on the concept of "wisdom" in the Greek culture.[13]

---

[13] "The Greeks vaunted in their alleged wisdom. Herodotus reported that these intellectual sophisticates had the reputation of 'pursuing every kind of knowledge' (*History* IV.77). Celsus (c. A.D. 178), a Greek philosopher who wrote a bitter diatribe against Christianity, characterized the followers of Jesus as those who eschewed wisdom, but who welcomed the senseless and the ignorant (see: Origen, *Against Celsus,*6:12-14). The Greeks viewed those outside the pale of Hellenism as 'barbarians' (cf. Rom. 1:14)."

The Christians in Corinth found their new ethics in conflict with what their neighbors claimed was the source of true wisdom. Especially in Corinth, the fledgling church was receiving pressure to continue the practices of the culture around them. Paul seeks to inform and reassure his spiritual children that true wisdom is from the Lord and they should expect it to clash with those who are not of the Lord.

A common mistake is to presume this passage is a contrast between the moral capacities of the "regenerate" and the "unregenerate," or the "natural man" versus the "spiritual man." Instead, the contrast is between the insufficiency of "human wisdom" versus power of "divine revelation" (or wisdom that is from man versus wisdom that is from God). Obviously, Paul felt the inspired Scriptures were sufficient to grant mankind the understanding for salvation, as he wrote to Timothy:

> **2 Timothy 3:15-16:** From childhood you have known the sacred writings which are able to give you the wisdom that leads to salvation through faith which is in Christ Jesus. All Scripture is inspired by God and profitable for teaching, for reproof, for correction, for training in righteousness.

Quote taken from: https://www.christiancourier.com/articles/643-who-is-the-natural-man-in-1-corinthians-2-14 [date accessed 5/6/17].

Paul's intention is to say that those who rely on human wisdom, instead of the spiritual truths brought by the inspired apostles, will see the cross as foolish and perish as a result. Paul is not saying that the natural man can only deem God's truth as foolish due to reasons beyond his control. Instead, he is explaining that those who trust in "human wisdom" instead of "divine revelation" will perish. This is why God is just to hold mankind accountable for how they respond to His appeals for reconciliation (John 12:48; 2 Cor. 5:20).

We begin on the wrong footing if we read the phrase "the word of the cross is foolishness to those who are perishing" (vs. 18) and assume that mankind's natural condition is somehow constrained to deem all divinely revealed truth as "foolish." God decided not which judgements each person would make about His word, but that he would be free to make them and thus by held justly responsible for either accepting or rejecting His clearly revealed truth.

Paul's overarching concern in this passage is to make a case for true wisdom as held in contrast with the "wisdom of the wise" (1:19), the "wisdom of this world" (1:20; 3:19), or the carnal "wisdom of men" (2:5). The Greeks boasted in their wisdom and Paul is providing them a spiritually inspired warning by teaching them what true divine wisdom looks like.

That wisdom is contained in the gospel revelation (1:24, 30; 2:7). There is nothing about that revelation that is insufficient in enabling a willing response (Rom. 1:16; John 20:31). Anyone who chooses to trade the clearly revealed truth in for lies stands as a fool "without excuse" (Rom. 1:20; Ps. 14:1).

Once a clear distinction is drawn between the wisdom of the world and heaven's wisdom, Paul moves on to speak of "the deep things of God" (vs. 10). Just as you cannot know what is in my mind unless I reveal it, so too, no one can access the "deep things of God" unless these mysteries are made known by His Spirit through the inspiration of the chosen apostles. Clearly, there are some deep mysteries kept hidden in the mind of God for a time. As the apostle Paul noted:

1 Corinthians 2:7-8: We declare God's wisdom, a mystery that has been hidden and that God destined for our glory before time began. None of the rulers of this age understood it, for if they had, they would not have crucified the Lord of glory.

It is only now, during the time of the apostles, that the mystery of Christ is being fully made known to all people. By what means? Some inner spiritual enlightenment? An effectual regenerative working? What does the Scripture tell us is the means God employed to help the world understand the depth of God's spiritual mysteries? Paul tells us plainly:

Ephesians 3:1-7: For this reason I, Paul, the prisoner of Christ Jesus for the sake of you

Gentiles— if indeed you have heard of the stewardship of God's grace which was given to me for you; that by revelation there was made known to me the mystery, as I wrote before in brief. By referring to this, *when you read you can understand my insight into the mystery of Christ, which in other generations was not made known to the sons of men, as it has now been revealed to His holy apostles and prophets in the Spirit;* to be specific, that the Gentiles are fellow heirs and fellow members of the body, and fellow partakers of the promise in Christ Jesus through the gospel, of which I was made a minister, according to the gift of God's grace which was given to me according to the working of His power (emphasis added).

Clearly, the means by which God assists mankind to understand the deep mysteries of spiritual truth is by inspiration of chosen messengers. As Paul writes in 1 Corinthians 2:13, "which things we also speak, not in words taught by human wisdom, but in those taught by the Spirit, combining spiritual thoughts with spiritual words."

The Holy Spirit revealed mysteries to "His holy apostles and prophets" and in turn, they write down "insight into the mystery of Christ" and "preach to the nations" so that the "wisdom of God might now be made known." There is absolutely nothing in all of Scripture that suggests that fallen humanity is unable to willingly respond to this gracious Holy Spirit-wrought truth of divine revelation calling all people to reconciliation from the fall!

With this in mind, let's focus on a key passage that is often misunderstood:

1 Corinthians 2:14: But a natural man does not accept the things of the Spirit of God, for they are foolishness to him; and he cannot understand them, because they are spiritually appraised.

Simply put, this passage can be taken to mean, "The man who freely chooses not to accept the things that come from the Spirit of God (apostles teaching, Scripture, etc.), but deem them as foolish, cannot understand spiritual truth, because those are the means of spiritual revelation."

This understanding of 1 Corinthians 2:14 becomes very simple when we answer the first question posed by this verse, "Why won't the natural man accept the things that come from the Spirit of God?" Paul is saying that the "natural man" is one who will not accept the wisdom from the Spirit of God because the man himself considers these things to be foolish by his own choosing, and he certainly could have chosen otherwise. Therefore, the lost man is incapable of ever understanding spiritual things unless and until he turns from human wisdom and accepts the wisdom being revealed by the Spirit through His chosen means (apostles, Scriptures, etc.).

How can any man understand something he has already deemed foolish in his heart? He cannot. Those who rely upon the wisdom of this age over and above the clear revelation of the Spirit cannot begin to understand the deep truths of God. This message seems to be the clear intention of the apostle.

The following verses support this line of reasoning as Paul goes on to confront the "carnal brethren" in Corinth as likewise being unable to receive these same "deep things of God" due to their carnality (3:1-3). The clear implication is that these believer's choices to live carnally, just like the unbeliever's choices to deem God's word as foolish, is the root cause of their inability to accept and understand deep spiritual meat of the apostle's teaching.

The believer's carnality, like the unbeliever's rejection of God's word, is a result of their own choosing. It is the responsibility of the believer to turn from carnality so as to receive the spiritual meat of God's word, just as it is the unbeliever's responsibility to turn from fleshly wisdom when confronted by the Holy Spirit-wrought truth of the gospel, "the power of God unto salvation" (Rom. 1:16).

Two views of rebellious men are in contrast here. On one view, man is born only morally able to reject God. On the other view, man knows God, is morally able to do differently, but chooses to reject God anyway. Which view of man makes him more morally culpable? Which

77

view makes man's rejections of God *worse*? Which view really demonstrates the justice of God?[14]

Even as we evaluate our own spiritual growth, it is tempting to see ourselves as unable to sin differently than we do. If spiritual truths, and therefore sanctified living, are out of our reach unless the Holy Spirit effectually changes us, then this can elevate our view of our own sin. In contrast, if God has already given us (through the gracious gifts of the indwelling Holy Spirit, Scripture, and discipleship) the sufficient capacities we need to live sanctified, and we *still* choose to live sinfully, then our sin is truly, deeply depraved. We cannot dismiss this contrast as a possible motivation for how we see the moral responsibility of man.

---

[14] See Appendix 3 on page 137 for more.

Chapter 9

By What Means Does God Make Himself Known?

At times theologians speak of mediated versus unmediated means of revelation. Unmediated is without anyone or anything intervening or acting as an intermediate. This is a direct form of revelation whereby God does not use any mediator. Sometimes throughout Scripture, God reveals himself in unmediated ways, as we see with Moses in Exodus 33:22. Today, however, we are more accustomed to God's use of mediated means (such as a Bible or a preacher).

How we apply God's means of communication (whether mediated or unmediated) to mankind's natural abilities to comprehend and accept *directly* revealed truth, is essential to this discussion. One could argue that reading or hearing the inspired word of God is a "mediated" (by way of means, or through a mediator) form of divine revelation. Shall we then assert that those means are insufficient to enable the natural man to respond freely to God's own chosen method of communication?

Should we believe that the Holy Spirit must do more than inspire the words (which clearly reveal truth and call us to reconciliation through faith) for us to have the ability to freely respond? I contend that this view is not convincingly established by the Scriptures.

God certainly uses a variety of means to communicate. That does not suggest, however, that some are sufficient and others are not. For instance, was the testimony of the witnesses to Christ's resurrection sufficient to allow Thomas to believe that Christ was alive even though he refused to do so? I believe it was. It was Thomas' own fault for not believing their testimony, not a lacking in the testimony or an inborn incapacity due to the sin of Adam. I blame Thomas alone for his refusal to believe in light of that clear mediated testimony. The fact that God chose to reveal Himself more directly (without a mediator) to Thomas was purely gracious; not required or necessary for a faith response. It must be established biblically that the proclaimed inspired truth is insufficient apart from some extra supernatural grace. I find no biblical evidence for this commonly held view.

Sometimes we can fail to recognize God's work through various means, especially if those means are more normative than supernatural. One popular analogy often used to illustrate this often misunderstood truth goes like this:

A very religious man was once caught in rising floodwaters. He climbed onto the roof of his house and trusted God to rescue him. A neighbor came by in a canoe and said, "The waters will soon be above your house. Hop in and we'll paddle to safety."

"No thanks" replied the religious man. "I've prayed to God and I'm sure he will save me"

A short time later the police came by in a boat. "The waters will soon be above your house. Hop in and we'll take you to safety."

"No thanks" replied the religious man. "I've prayed to God and I'm sure he will save me"

A little time later a rescue services helicopter hovered overhead, let down a rope ladder and said. "The waters will soon be above your house. Climb the ladder and we'll fly you to safety."

"No thanks" replied the religious man. "I've prayed to God and I'm sure he will save me"

All this time the floodwaters continued to rise, until soon they reached above the roof and the religious man drowned. When he arrived at heaven he demanded an audience with God. Ushered into God's throne room he said, "Lord, why am I here in heaven? I prayed for you to save me, I trusted you to save me from that flood."

"Yes you did my child" replied the Lord. "And I sent you a canoe, a boat and a helicopter. But you never got in."[15]

God works through human means and there is no biblical reason to suggest those means are insufficient to accomplish God's purpose. The canoe, boat and helicopter like the Scriptures, preachers and the inborn conscience are sufficient means God has employed to accomplish a given purpose. There is no good reason to dismiss these means as not being enough to enable a positive response simply because a large mass of people choose not to respond positively to those given means.

THE APOSTLE'S TEACHINGS ARE MEDIATED MEANS

Would you affirm or deny this claim:

The gospel, brought by unmediated revelation to His chosen apostles, is insufficient to enable the belief of their hearers. Therefore, God must also reveal that same truth to each hearer individually by the same unmediated means He used to bring that revelation to the apostles in the first place.

I see no biblical reason to affirm this statement. The apostles received unmediated revelation and were commissioned with the specific purpose of spreading what they were told. Must God also give that same unmediated revelation to every hearer of the gospel? If

---

[15] Quote taken from: https://storiesforpreaching.com/i-sent-you-a-rowboat/ [date accessed: 01/05/19].

so, where is this taught in Scripture? Why even use the mediated means of the apostle's writings if those means are not sufficient anyway? Why not just reveal truth directly (unmediated) to each individual to begin with and cut out the apparently insufficient "middleman"?

If unmediated revelation is required for salvation then the apostles' mission to preach, teach, and author Spirit-inspired letters was impotent to accomplish its Christ-commissioned purpose. We must maintain that God's use of both mediated and unmediated means are sufficient to accomplish their biblically stated purpose unless the Bible itself clearly says otherwise.

GOD'S UNMEDIATED PRESENCE IS CONDITIONAL

Christians do enjoy the Holy Spirit's unmediated presence. However, God's personal activity comes as a result of a faith response to God's inspired appeal, not the other way around. The gospel is God's appeal for us to have a personal/direct "unmediated" encounter with God. To suggest God must encounter us in that direct/unmediated way for us to freely respond to an appeal to do so seems to get the proverbial cart before the horse.

Consider another analogy. If a sworn enemy sends me a letter requesting to meet in person to be reconciled, does that enemy need to personally hand deliver this letter to enable a willing response? Of course not. A courier can carry the letter and it would still sufficiently communicate the intent of that enemy and the means by which we can be reconciled. Why would God's chosen means be less sufficient? Where does the Bible explicitly teach that such inspired means are not sufficient to enable a free response?

Jesus does indeed enlighten every man (1 John 1:9). But by what means? Each man and woman did not receive the unmediated revelation that the apostles got when writing the Scripture. So, I agree that God enlightens every man, but He does so through His chosen means. (See Eph. 3:1-10)

GOD'S MEDIATED MEANS ARE SUFFICIENT

The crux of this discussion centers upon the sufficiency of God's inspired truth to enable a free response. The condition of enjoying the Holy Spirit's unmediated presence is sufficiently enabled by His chosen mediated means. To be clear, I do not believe that the message of the gospel produces faith in its hearer. Instead, the gospel enables the hearer to freely respond in faith. I affirm the Holy Spirit's unmediated presence and continual influence but do so while maintaining the sufficiency of how He has chosen to reveal Himself and His inspired truth. In other words, I see no biblical reason to believe that God's unmediated presence and influence somehow suggests that His work through mediated means is insufficient to accomplish its given purpose.

The Holy Spirit continues to work to preserve and carry His word by means of inspired Holy Spirit-indwelled messengers. The Holy Spirit is the wielder or carrier of the word. When Paul wrote "the sword of the Spirit, which is the word of God" (Eph. 6:17), he illustrated this concept perfectly. When the word of God comes, in any of its forms (people, Scripture, nature, etc.), it is a work of the Spirit "wielding it."

You can look at every instance of the word coming and see that it is always tied through the work of the Spirit. We cannot assume the gospel's preservation and continued dispersion would have happened apart from the continual work of the Spirit through His Bride. I am not making a case that the gospel would have continued to accomplish its intended purposes absent the Holy Spirit's work in other ways. My goal is to illustrate the sufficiency of the inspired word in enabling the lost to respond to its appeal.

For instance, in your hands is the mediated means of a book written to explain my theological perspective. Is this book sufficient to communicate to you, the reader, so that you may understand and possibly adopt my perspective? If you were to come over to my house tomorrow to further discuss these matters in an "unmediated" manner, would that suggest that this book was no longer sufficient to convince readers of my perspective? Of course not. I am not sure why it would be any different with God's chosen means of communication with fallen humanity.

So, it is not that hearing the message certainly produces faith, but that it enables a free response of faith. The gospel enables the lost man to place his trust in Jesus (Rom. 10:14). That is important in this discussion because the burden here is not to reveal that hearing divinely inspired truth is sufficient to save the lost, but only that it is sufficient to enable a free response of those who are lost. One cannot conflate the responsibility of the lost to respond to God's revelation and the gracious choice of God to save and indwell those who freely believe that revelation, as He promised to do.

Chapter 10

Can Enslaved Sinners Confess They Are In Bondage?

God's Provision Sets Captives Free

What effect does sin have on the hearing and believing the gospel? According to Scripture, all sinners are enslaved to sin, but does that mean all sinners are incapable of confessing that fact in light of God's gracious revelation through the law and the gospel?

All people are slaves to sin, but that is why God sent truth which may set man free (John 8:32). I see no biblical reason to suggest that God's inspired truth is insufficient to do just that.

Romans 10:14-15: How, then, can they call on the one they have not believed in? And how can they believe in the one of whom they have not heard? And how can they hear without someone preaching to them? And how can anyone preach unless they are sent?

The apostles were, for the first time, being sent to proclaim these deep hidden spiritual truths, which the lost world could not have believed unless someone told them (Rom. 10:14).

2 Corinthians 3:15-16: Even to this day when Moses is read, a veil covers their hearts. But whenever anyone turns to the Lord, the veil is taken away.

We cannot get the order incorrect by insisting that God removes the veil so as compel one to turn to the Lord, when the text clearly indicates that it is by turning to the Lord (and His clear revelation brought by inspiration) that one may understand so as to have the veil (the misapplication of God's law) removed.

The Scriptures teach that mankind, while sinners, may "become hardened" or "grow calloused" (Acts 28:27-28) or be given over to their desires so as to become defiled (Rom. 1; Eph. 4:17-19). This is a potential for every lost sinner who continues to harden their hearts toward the light of divine revelation, as was the case with most Israelites of the New Testament.

Many theologians misapply some of the teachings about the calloused condition of man once "given over" to their depraved and calloused wills as if it applies to an innate condition from birth. There must be a distinction drawn between the heart of a sinner and the heart of a hardened sinner.

Acts 28:27-28: 'For this people's heart has become calloused; they hardly hear with their ears, and they have closed their eyes. Otherwise they might see with their eyes, hear with their ears, understand with their hearts and turn, and I would heal them.' 'Therefore I want you to know that God's salvation has been sent to the Gentiles, and they will listen!'

What might they have done had they not "become calloused" according to the Scripture above? "Otherwise they might see with their eyes, hear with their ears, understand with their hearts and turn." Notice the contrast with the Gentiles (while still sinful) who will listen. What is the distinction Paul is drawing between the Jews and the Gentiles in this text? One is calloused and thus unable to turn while the other, who are still sinners, are willing (generally speaking) to listen and respond.

Both the Jews and the Gentiles are equally culpable for being sinful (Rom. 1-3). Both Jews and Gentiles are not equally calloused in their self-righteousness, which is what makes it so difficult for the Pharisaical Israelites (old wine skins, Mark 2:22) to accept God's clear revelation.

Why do you suppose Jesus referred to a child as an example of what we must emulate to enter His kingdom (Matt. 18:3)? What is the difference in the condition of a child's heart and the heart of an older person? Are they both equally "hardened" from birth as some doctrines seems to impose onto the text? Clearly not. The heart of a child who has reached an age of accountability, [16] while culpable for sin, has not yet grown calloused and stubborn in his rebellion. A child, like the Gentiles referenced above, "will listen" because they are able to "see with their eyes, hear with their ears, understand with their heart and turn" so as to be healed (Acts 28:27-28). They are still sinners who are in need of a Savior, but they have not yet grown so calloused that they cannot respond positively to God's own appeals.

---

[16] Scriptures do not speak so much about a specific age but simply to a time in everyone's life when God's truth is clearly made known. When a child comes to understand that they have sinned against God and deserve punishment due to their sins, then and only then can they give an account of their wrongdoings. This is why we reference them being as being "accountable" (able to give an account for sin) or "responsible" (able to respond to Christ's appeal). Some even prefer the "age of responsibility" because it connotes the child's ability-to-respond of his own volition to the words of Christ, after all, every one of us will be judged by those very words (John 12:48). Christ indicates that one's accountability depends, at least in part, upon one's understanding of sin (John 9:41, 15:22). Paul likewise seems to indicate this same principle in Rom. 7:9-10. Jesus also spoke of allowing the children to come to him "for such is the kingdom of heaven" (Lk 18:16). And Jesus even uses a child as an example in one of his lessons declaring, "Anyone who becomes humble as this little child is the greatest in the Kingdom of Heaven." King David seems to presume that one day he would be reunited with his child who died in infancy (2 Sam. 12:22-23). Also, when God banned the unfaithful Israelites from entering the promised land he did so based upon age and ignorance (Dt. 1:39) Likewise, when the prophet Isaiah foretold of the Messiah's coming he spoke of when a boy "will know enough to refuse evil and choose good," suggesting there is a time in the child's life he remains without enough knowledge to make accountable moral choices (Isa. 7:16). So too, the prophet Ezekiel seems to strongly indicate that guilt was not imputed from one's parents, which would seem to contradict the idea that all people are born guilty for the sins of those who have come before him (Ezek. 18:20).

CONSIDER THIS ANALOGY

Suppose an alcoholic man is finally confronted by all his friends and family about his addiction. They schedule an intervention and confront him boldly about his poor choices and how it has affected every aspect of his life. At first, he tells them that he is fine and that he can stop drinking anytime he wants. They all insist this is not true and continue to point out all the times that he had tried to quit but could not. After hours of back and forth, his teenage daughter finally enters into the conversation. After hearing his daughter's emotional and loving plea, he finally breaks down weeping. He confesses his addiction and accepts the help that the group offers by checking into a rehab facility.

Is it true that this man was an addict and a slave to alcohol? Yes. Is it true that this man still had the ability to humbly admit his addiction and accept the help that was offered? Yes. Both are true. The alcoholic, like every sinner, is in bondage, yet he is still capable of owning up to that problem so as to receive the needed help. Similarly, we are all *sinaholics*, but we are all still responsible to "humble ourselves" just as the Scriptures call us to do over and over again without qualification.

Imagine what would happen if one of the family members of the alcoholic insisted that his addiction to alcohol equaled his inability to willingly accept the help being offered? Besides possibly squelching the group's desire to even confront and try to convince the man to confess his addiction, they would have to realize that the only solution would be to incapacitate him in some manner and throw him in the rehab facility regardless of his willingness to go. Or, if that was too violent, I guess they could have drugged him somehow to make his desires change so that he would willingly check into the facility. It is only when they insist that he is unable to freely admit his bondage to alcohol after being lovingly confronted that newly invented solutions must be offered (i.e., effectual calls or irresistible grace or pre-faith regeneration — none of which are explicitly expounded upon by any biblical authors or early church fathers).

Many well-intending theologians have simply conflated the concept of bondage to sin (addiction) with a moral incapacity to humble oneself and confess that enslaved condition so as to receive the help that is being offered (responsibility). But, affirming that all people are slaves to sin is not equal to affirming that all people are morally incapable of humbly confessing that fact when the truth is made clearly known. Slavery to sin is not equal to the moral inability to confess our enslavement in response to God's loving provision and powerful Holy Spirit-inspired appeals for reconciliation.

SUMMARY

God's provision is sufficient to enable lost souls to be found. The Scriptures do not teach us that the fall of mankind resulted in the moral incapacity to respond positively to God's revelation. The good news is that God's grace is available to all who respond willingly to it. The grace of the gospel does not take an extra working of grace to work. This once mysterious truth about Jesus, hidden in times past, is now known. It has been made known through God's chosen messengers.

These messengers, the apostles, wrote letters proclaiming the sufficiency of God's revelation to enable a response. Being enslaved to sin and blinded by the wisdom of this world does not render the unbeliever morally unable to admit they are enslaved and blinded. Indeed, Scripture claims the enabling of belief to be the very purpose for which it is written and sent to all people (John 20:31).

Chapter 11

Why Does God Provide The Gospel To All?

God Provides because God is Good

Good people are typically recognized as being good because of their willingness to impartially provide good things to others. They are not doing this because it is required by law, but simply on the basis of their good and benevolent character. God is also recognizably good in this same way. He provides good things to others indiscriminately, not because He has to, but simply on the basis of His good character. This goodness is also seen in the fact that He does not show favoritism to one person over another for no apparent reason.

WHAT IS FAVORITISM OR PARTIALITY?

Partiality is an unfair bias in favor of one thing or person compared with another. Favoritism is the practice of giving unfair preferential treatment to one person or group at the expense of another.[17]

So, what does it mean to say God is not partial or that He does not practice favoritism? Does it mean God cannot select certain individuals for a certain purpose? No. According to the definitions above, there must be an unfair bias or a preferential treatment at the expense of another in order for it to be considered unjust partiality or favoritism.

For instance, suppose a man has five children. Would it be unfair to select one of the children to deliver a message to the rest of them? Of course not. His choice of one child to accomplish this chore is not at the expense of the other children nor is there some kind of bias which shows this child as being unfairly favored over the others.

But suppose the man selects one of the children to deliver a message and then rewards that child with a piece of cake for his efforts once the task is complete. Is this biased favoritism? No. The other children have not suffered a loss due to the father's choices and rewards.

In the same way, God's choice of Israel and certain Israelites to carry His message and to receive the blessings He gives to those who accomplish His assigned

---

[17] *The Oxford Pocket Dictionary of Current English*, (New York: Oxford University Press, 2009). Quote taken from: https://www.ency-clopedia.com/humanities/ dictionaries-thesauruses-pictures-and-press-releases/partiality [date accessed: 12/14/18].

tasks is not partiality or favoritism. It is simply God's chosen means to bless all the families of the earth (Gen. 12:3).

PARTIALITY AND FAVORITISM ILLUSTRATED

Suppose a high school principal selected twelve of his seniors to spread a message to the student body about a special treat being given out in the cafeteria. Would the principal's choice of these twelve messengers demonstrate that he has favorites or has unfairly shown partiality to some individuals over others? No. He has chosen these messengers to bring a blessing to the entire student body and his selection of one student to serve as a messenger over another student is not in any way to the detriment or neglect of that student who was not chosen for this task.

We believe this is what God has done with the gospel. He has selected from Israel (like the senior class) messengers to bless all the world (the entire student body). Here are a few biblical passages which indicate this:

Acts 10:40-42: God raised him from the dead on the third day and caused him to be seen. He was not seen by all the people, but by witnesses whom God had already chosen—by us who ate and drank with him after he rose from the dead. He commanded us to preach to the people and to testify that he is the one whom God appointed as judge of the living and the dead.

Acts 13:47: For this is what the Lord has commanded us: "I have made you a light for the Gentiles, that you may bring salvation to the ends of the earth."

Mark 16:15: He said to them (Jewish apostles), "Go into all the world and preach the gospel to all creation."

John 15:16: (Speaking to his chosen apostles) You did not choose me, but I chose you and appointed you so that you might go and bear fruit—fruit that will last.

As mentioned before, this is all a fulfillment of God's original covenant with Abraham:

Gen 12:2-3: And I will make you a great nation, And I will bless you, And make your name great; And so you shall be a blessing; And I will bless those who bless you, And the one who curses you I will curse. And in you all the families of the earth will be blessed.

But suppose the high school, in our analogy above, was bilingual and most of the students only spoke and understood Spanish. And what if this principal only selected English-speaking messengers to take the message to the entire student body, knowing full well that only the English-speaking students would hear and understand the news about the blessing he made available in the cafeteria.

Suppose that the principal only bought enough treats for his English-speaking students and so his intention was for only them to hear and understand the message. He did not want to appear biased so he told the messengers to invite the entire student body but secretly he knew only the English-speaking students would understand the message and respond.

Does that indicate an unfair bias or partiality? Of course it does. Now, did the principal owe any of the students these treats? No. No one is saying he did. But for him to outwardly pretend as if he wished for the entire student body to be blessed while secretly only purchasing treats for some and sending a message that was intended only for some to understand is clearly showing favoritism and an unjust bias. But we know that God does not show favoritism, as the Scriptures clearly teach:

Psalm 9:8: And He will judge the world in righteousness; He will execute judgment for the peoples with equity.

Psalm 98:9: For He is coming to judge the earth; He will judge the world with righteousness And the peoples with equity.

Jeremiah 17:10: I the Lord search the heart and examine the mind, to reward each person according to their conduct, according to what their deeds deserve.

Jeremiah 11:20: But you, Lord Almighty, who judge righteously and test the heart and mind, let me see your vengeance on them, for to you I have committed my cause.

Genesis 18:25: Far be it from you to do such a thing, to slay the righteous with the wicked, so that the righteous and the wicked are treated alike. Far be it from you! Shall not the Judge of all the earth deal justly?

Job 8:1-6: Then Bildad the Shuhite replied: "How long will you say such things? Your words are a blustering wind. Does God pervert justice? Does the Almighty pervert what is right? When your children sinned against him, he gave them over to the penalty of their sin. But if you will seek God earnestly and plead with the Almighty, if you are pure and upright, even now he will rouse himself on your behalf and restore you to your prosperous state."

Luke 20:21: They questioned Him, saying, "Teacher, we know that You speak and teach correctly, and You are not partial to any, but teach the way of God in truth."

CONFLATING GOD'S CHOICES

Clearly, God does choose certain individuals through whom to reveal Himself and His word. He obviously inspires them in a way that He does not with everyone else. There is a measure of grace uniquely given to His chosen messengers (Eph. 3:1-7; Acts 10:41). If this was required to be saved, however, then a strong case could be made against God's impartiality. But, if these messengers are chosen to bring a blessing to all people then no charge of injustice or biased favoritism could stand. Only if one conflates God's choice of messengers with His choice of those blessed by that message could it be argued that God is impartial or unfair.

While God does make selections of certain individuals for honorable tasks, the Scriptures are clear that God does not show partiality with people regarding such significant matters as their judgment, their salvation, or their condemnation (Deut. 10:17; 2 Chron. 19:7; Job 33:12-30; 34:17-27; Matt. 22:16; Mark 12:14; Luke 20:21; Acts 10:34-35; Rom. 1:16-21; 2:8-11; Gal. 2:6; Eph. 6:9; 1 Peter 1:17).

Deuteronomy 10:17: For the LORD your God is the God of gods and the Lord of lords, the great, the mighty, and the awesome God who does not show partiality nor take a bribe.

The word here for partiality is *nasa'*, and has a variety of meanings, but all with the same implication. It means to lift up, carry, support, or even to take away or forgive.

The Lord does not unfairly lift one person to the expense of another. God is most glorified not at the expense of His creation, but at the expense of Himself for the sake of His creation.

2 Chronicles 19:7: Now then let the fear of the LORD be upon you; be very careful what you do, for the LORD our God will have no part in unrighteousness or partiality or the taking of a bribe.

This is the same word (*nasa'*), and notice it is put right in line with unrighteousness. To be partial, or show favoritism, is to be unrighteous.

Matthew 22:16: And they sent their disciples to Him, along with the Herodians, saying, "Teacher, we know that You are truthful and teach the way of God in truth, and defer to no one; for You are not partial to any."

Christ teaches the way of God in truth. Notice what it says: He teaches truth, and does not defer to anyone (in teaching the truth), for He is not partial to any.

Mark 12:14: They came and said to Him, "Teacher, we know that You are truthful and defer to no one; for You are not partial to any, but teach the way of God in truth."

Acts 10:34-35: Then Peter began to speak: "I now realize how true it is that God does not show favoritism but accepts from every nation the one who fears him and does what is right."

God does not accept certain people based upon their morality or nationality but accepts any and all who fear Him and trust in His provision.

Romans 2:8-11: But for those who are self-seeking and who reject the truth and follow evil, there will be wrath and anger. There will be trouble and distress for every human being who does evil: first for the Jew, then for the Gentile; but glory, honor and peace for everyone who does good: first for the Jew, then for the Gentile. For God does not show favoritism.

God's wrath (or trouble and distress) comes upon those who are self-seeking and reject the truth so as to follow evil.

Galatians 2:6: But from those who were of high reputation (what they were makes no difference to me; God shows no partiality)—well, those who were of reputation contributed nothing to me.

Ephesians 6:9: And masters, do the same things to them, and give up threatening, knowing that both their Master and yours is in heaven, and there is no partiality with Him.

1 Peter 1:17: If you address as Father the One who impartially judges according to each one's work, conduct yourselves in fear during the time you stay on earth.

God has also commanded all to be like Him, impartial, not showing favoritism in judgment and instruction (Ex. 23:2-4; Lev. 19:15; Deut. 1:17; 16:9; 2 Chron. 19:7; Job 13:8-10; 32:21-22; Prov. 28:21; Mal. 2:9; Eph. 6:9; 1 Tim. 5:21; James 2:21; 4:8-9).

Exodus 23:2-4: You shall not follow the masses in doing evil, nor shall you testify in a dispute so as to turn aside after a multitude in order to pervert justice; nor shall you be partial to a poor man in his dispute.

Leviticus 19:15: You shall do no injustice in judgment; you shall not be partial to the poor nor defer to the great, but you are to judge your neighbor fairly.

Deuteronomy 1:17: You shall not show partiality in judgment; you shall hear the small and the great alike. You shall not fear man, for the judgment is God's.

Deuteronomy 16:19: You shall not distort justice; you shall not be partial, and you shall not take a bribe, for a bribe blinds the eyes of the wise and perverts the words of the righteous.

Job 13:8-10: Will you show partiality for Him? Will you contend for God? Will it be well when He examines you? Or will you deceive Him as one deceives a man? He will surely reprove you If you secretly show partiality.

Job 32:21-22: Let me now be partial to no one, Nor flatter any man. For I do not know how to flatter, Else my Maker would soon take me away.

Proverbs 28:21: To show partiality is not good, Because for a piece of bread a man will transgress.

Malachi 2:9: So I also have made you despised and abased before all the people, just as you are not keeping My ways but are showing partiality in the instruction.

Israel as a kingdom of priests was showing partiality in teaching God's word, and thus God judged them. God is not a hypocrite. His judgment is based upon His own character and therefore we can know that He does not show partiality in judgment or instruction.

1 Timothy 5:21: I solemnly charge you in the presence of God and of Christ Jesus and of His chosen angels, to maintain these principles without bias, doing nothing in a spirit of partiality.

James 2:1: My brothers and sisters, believers in our glorious Jesus Christ must not show favoritism.

James 2:4: Have you not made distinctions among yourselves, and become judges with evil motives?

James 2:8-9: If you really keep the royal law found in Scripture, "Love your neighbor as yourself," you are doing right. But if you show favoritism, you sin and are convicted by the law as lawbreakers.

James 3:17: But the wisdom that comes from heaven is first of all pure; then peace-loving, considerate, submissive, full of mercy and good fruit, impartial and sincere.

Chapter 12

Why Should We Evangelize?

God's Provision is Persuasive

Persuasion is at the very heart of apologetics, and I dare say, it is at the heart of evangelism itself. What does the Bible say about persuasion? Let us look at some of its most relevant uses:

Acts 17:4: Some of the Jews were persuaded and joined Paul and Silas.

Acts 18:4: Every Sabbath he reasoned in the synagogue, trying to persuade Jews and Greeks.

Acts 18:13: This man persuades men to worship God.

Acts 19:8: [Paul was] arguing persuasively about the kingdom of God.

Acts 26:28: Do you think that in such a short time you can persuade me to become a Christian?

Acts 28:23-24: They arranged to meet Paul on a certain day, and came in even larger numbers to the place where he was staying. He witnessed to them from morning till evening, explaining about the kingdom of God, and from the Law of Moses and from the Prophets he tried to persuade them about Jesus. Some were convinced by what he said, but others would not believe.

2 Corinthians 5:11: Since, then, we know what it is to fear the Lord, we try to persuade others.

Too often we speak only of the need to proclaim and explain the good news to the lost, but clearly, the Bible teaches us that we should be trying to persuade people of its truthfulness. Is that not what evangelism and apologetics are all about?

Notice in Acts 17, when Paul "dialogued" (the Greek word dialegomai, meaning "reasoned") in the synagogue that it resulted in people being "persuaded" (Greek: peitho). Paul explained the Old Testament Scriptures and answered their questions to convince them of the truth. This was typical in his approach with his fellow Jews ("his custom" v. 2) because he knew the Jews considered their Scriptures to be authoritative.

However, Paul's approach with the Gentiles shifted to speaking about their culture first rather than the Scriptures because that is what they viewed as authoritative or most influential (see vs. 22-31). Paul is using his God-given gift of persuasion by connecting with his audience on their level. He has "become all things to all people so that by all possible means [he] might save some" (1 Cor. 9:22). This, of course, is still something for which we praise God because He is the one who enabled Paul with this ability.

WHAT DOES IT MEAN TO PERSUADE?

Vine's *Dictionary of New Testament Words* describes the word "persuade" as follows:

> To prevail upon or win over, to bring about a change of mind by the influence of reason or moral considerations.[18]

Notice this definition draws attention to both reason and morality. In other words, appealing to one's conscience in an effort to get them to do what is right morally may be one effective approach to persuasion, but it's not the only tool. Appealing to sound reason (by means of dialogue) is an equally important biblical tool in the persuasion process.

Persuasion is not about emotionally abusing people into submission. It is about speaking the truth in love (Eph. 4:15). It is about being a person of character who earns the respect of the audience by showing them respect. It is about making sound, logical, well-reasoned arguments that connect with the listener on a personal level. As Paul said:

---

[18] "Persuade." *Vine's Expository Dictionary of New Testament Words.* Quote taken from: https://studybible.info /vines/Persuade [date accessed 11/12/28].

2 Corinthians 4:2: We have renounced secret and shameful ways; we do not use deception, nor do we distort the word of God. On the contrary, by setting forth the truth plainly we commend ourselves to every man's conscience in the sight of God.

Paul, while he was in Ephesus, was "arguing persuasively" (Acts 19:8). Does not that strongly imply that it is possible to argue "unpersuasively"? Why would anyone want to risk being unpersuasive when it comes to proclaiming the most important news of all?

WHY PREACH AND TRY TO PERSUADE THE LOST IF THEY ALREADY KNOW THE TRUTH?

Just because someone knows something is true by means of natural revelation or conscience does not mean we should leave them alone. If you have taught your child something, and he knows it and goes against it, do you leave him alone? No, you go to him again, teach him again, and persuade him to do the right thing. So it is with God and His own gracious means to continually and patiently reach out to his creation again and again. God says,

Isaiah 65:2-3: I have spread out My hands all day long to a rebellious people, Who walk in the way which is not good, following their own thoughts, A people who continually provoke Me to My face. (Also quoted by Paul in Rom. 10:21.)

They knew the truth already and rebelled. This is like all of us. But yet the Lord still calls, and holds out His hands, and sends His Spirit to convict, reproof, and call them to repentance. That is what we are to do as well. We call all those who have squandered away the inheritance the Lord purchased for all men and plead with them to repent and follow Him. Do not be like Israel, who was freed, but yet rebelled and went back to bondage and did not enter His rest. We are called as just one of many vessels to spread the light that God has continually brought to all men.

God desires all men to be saved. He takes no pleasure in the death of the wicked. He is patient with us, desiring all come to repentance. Why then, are not all saved? Because He has given us the choice.

Deuteronomy 30:19: I call heaven and earth to witness against you today, that I have set before you life and death, the blessing and the curse. So choose life in order that you may live.

God provides all of us with the knowledge by which we may be saved, but there are also consequences for rejecting Him if we choose to suppress that truth. He gives His witness to us through creation and through what He has sown into our hearts. This is to persuade us to trust in Him.

Likewise, He provides further witness through His written and spoken word. All these divine means are witnesses sent to persuade men to trust in Him. Just because one method fails to work on any particular individual does not mean we should give up hope and stop trying! We should persist in persuading because we know what it means to fear the Lord (2 Cor. 5:11).

If your neighbor hears the gospel at a church service and has not trusted in the Lord, do you just let him be? He already knows "what to do," so what is the point in trying to persuade him further? That is not how the apostles reasoned, and it certainly should not be how we reason either. I hope you go to your neighbor in love and share God's provision in order to persuade him or her to believe and trust in the Lord for salvation.

Israel knew the Lord and knew how to be saved, yet the Lord continued to send them prophets and divine messages to persuade them to repent. They knew what God required, but God still raised up prophets to send them, knowing that many of those prophets would be killed delivering the same message they already knew.

We can and should reiterate the wonderful good news to people who may be hardening their hearts or suppressing the truth in unrighteousness. We can and should reiterate that they are sinners and that they will be judged, something they all intuitively know already (Rom. 1:32). We can plead with them and persuade them to repent and trust in the Lord. We can strive to tear down strongholds that may have been built up (2 Cor. 10:4). We can appeal to apologetic arguments and sound reason. We can plead with them to repent so as to be saved because that is the example we see in Scripture (Acts 28:23).

We do so because we sincerely believe God provided atonement for everyone and desires for all to repent so as to be saved. We persist in our efforts to persuade the lost because we love God, love them and do not want any to perish.

Men may choose to suppress the truth (Rom. 1:18) or harden their hearts (Heb. 3:15). They may become callous in their unrighteousness (Eph. 4:19). But, we preach and teach because we are in service to the Lord. We want to be a tool the Spirit uses to shine the Light, to bring the truth, to soften men's hearts because we believe the truth may set them free (John 8:32).

Some may say, "But people have died in proclaiming the gospel, why die to proclaim something people already know?" To persuade men to repent and trust in the Lord and to follow the model of Christ's sacrificial love for His enemies (Luke 14:26; John 15:13). The Israelites of the Old Testament knew the message of salvation. They knew that if they trusted in the Lord, He would forgive them and cover them in grace. But they rebelled. They all knew the message, but they suppressed the truth and did not listen. God raised up prophets, and commanded them to go to these rebellious people who already knew the message and to tell them the message again and again, and often these prophets were killed

(Neh. 9:26; Matt. 23:34, 37; Acts 7:52). They went because they loved God, loved people, and wanted to persuade people to repent and obey the gospel. Paul's kinsmen (the physical Israelites) rejected it, and Paul had so much love he would have accursed himself to save some of them (Rom. 9:1-4).

Conclusion

When we call God "good" we mean that He is "recognizably good," which is based on standards revealed to us in the Scriptures. The news about God is called the "Gospel" (good news) because God's character is loving, kind, patient, impartial, just, right and clearly made known. In short the truth about God is good because He is good... recognizably good.

Those who selflessly provide for others in need are called "good" for a reason and it is for this same reason that we call God "good." We are not saying this out of obligation or fear of punishment, but because we recognize His goodness by what He does. A biblically recognizable characteristic of goodness is one's willingness to provide for those in need and that is what God does though His Son, Jesus Christ.

Though we believe God's ways can be mysterious at times, we maintain that questionable instances revealed to us in the Scripture can be reasonably explained as consistent with His good character. The Bible clearly demonstrates the loving character of a God who treats His creation in a recognizably good way; a God who does not arbitrarily play favorites or show biased partiality; a God who makes Himself known in a clear and believable way; a God who is not most glorified at the expense of His creation, but at the expense of Himself for the sake of His creation; a God who demonstrates His love by providing the means of salvation for every individual, not because He has to, but because of who He is!

Appendix 1

What is the Difference Between the Labels Traditionalism, Arminianism and Provisionism?

People sometimes ask questions about the various labels used to delineate a particular theological perspective. Admittedly, this can get quite confusing as theologians are rarely content with the labels ascribed to their given perspective and no theological worldview is monolithic with complete unity among all scholars ascribing to its respective label. I would like to briefly give some explanation surrounding the labels used in reference to my particular perspective.

TRADITIONALISM[19]

In 2001, Fisher Humphreys and Paul E. Robertson wrote *God So Loved the World: Traditional Baptists and Calvinism*. When these two irenic professors used the term *traditional* in their book, there was no outcry, for everyone grasped the fact that they were using the term to describe the most widely accepted Southern Baptist view of salvation. Sometimes referred to as *Whosoever Will* doctrine (in reference to John 3:16's obviously inclusive connotations) this was the view taught by

---

[19] Some of the commentary in this section was used by permission from the connect316.net website, which is no longer available.

Herschel Hobbs, Adrian Rogers, and most notable Southern Baptist scholars since around the 1920s and 30s when the SBC began its growth to become the largest Protestant denomination in the world.

In 2012, another effort was made to define what most Southern Baptists believed about salvation in light of the growing popularity of Calvinism within the convention. A document was drafted, whose primary author was Eric Hankins, entitled *A Statement of the Traditional Southern Baptist Understanding of God's Plan of Salvation.* The word *traditional* was again used for the basic Baptist view held by a majority within the Southern Baptist Convention (SBC) for the last one hundred years or so.

Some have objected to the term Traditionalism, misunderstanding it as an attempt to claim the *Whosoever Will* tradition as the only tradition in Southern Baptist life. Of course, it is not the only tradition, and that is not something the label is meant to communicate. Calling something "traditional" does not necessarily mean "how it began," but merely "the way things have been for a very long time." For instance, we often refer to music of our grandparents or parent's generation as "traditional worship," but that does not necessarily mean all Southern Baptist churches started with that music style. So, the intention of this label was not to offend or mislead anyone. It was just a reference point to try and identify the theological distinctions within Southern Baptist life.

Some insist that the Southern Baptist Convention was started primarily by Calvinists, so that is the real "tradition." There is some truth to this claim, but the SBC has changed dramatically in its faith and practice since the times of the Civil War. The fact is that the convention's overwhelming growth to become the largest protestant denomination was under the more traditionalistic understanding of soteriology.

Others have objected to the term *Traditionalism* on the basis that it must favor old-fashioned forms of worship, dress, and ministry. To be a *Traditionalist*, in their view, is to be an old, washed-up fogey whose theology and ministry is out of place in today's world. Once again, this definition is simply a caricature of the term's true meaning.

Still others object to the term because it limits itself to being tied to the SBC when many adherents are not necessarily associated with an SBC church or entity. I completely understand and even share some of these concerns regarding the label *Traditionalism*.

ARMINIANISM

I've often told people that I am not an Arminian, but that is not because I dislike Arminians; nor is it because I disagree with them over that many issues. In fact, Traditional Southern Baptists agree with much of what many good Arminian brothers teach. But there are several differences I have with my Arminian friends that

119

should be noted. For instance, some classical Arminians have various views on the doctrine of Eternal Security and Apostasy than what is typically held by a *traditional* Southern Baptist.

Another point of distinction involves Arminian adherence to the doctrine of "Total Inability." Now, even among *Traditional* Baptists, there exist various nuances over the nature of fallen humanity in response to God's revelation. However, the *Traditional* statement, signed by many notable *Traditional* scholars, clearly denounces the concept of "Total Inability," a view maintained by all Calvinists and many classical Arminian scholars.

"Total Inability" is the belief that all humanity is born incapable of willingly coming to Christ for salvation even in light of the Holy Spirit-wrought truth of the Gospel, unless God graciously works to empower the will of lost man (effectually by way of regeneration for the Calvinist, and sufficiently by way of "prevenient grace" for the Arminian). Typically, *Traditionalists* do not accept the unfounded presumption that the libertarian freedom of man's will was lost due to the fall. As article two of the Traditional statement says,

> We deny that Adam's sin resulted in the incapacitation of any person's free will or rendered any person guilty before he has personally sinned.

Those affirming the Traditional Statement seem to be affirming along with me that humanity did not lose the moral capacity to respond positively to God or His truth.

Responding to an Arminian

I have much respect for the scholarship and work of Dr. Roger Olson, a notable Arminian theologian. I have used his resources many times in my own studies and find him to be a thoughtful and thoroughly biblical scholar in all respects. He unashamedly wears the label "Arminian" and defends his views as well as I have ever seen. However, I do differ with him regarding the Arminian doctrine known as "Prevenient Grace." Dr. Olson explains it this way:

> *Prevenient Grace* is simply a term for the grace of God that goes before, prepares the way, enables, assists the sinner's repentance and faith (conversion). According to classical Calvinism this prevenient grace is always efficacious and given only to the elect through the gospel; it effects conversion. According to classical Arminianism it is an operation of the Holy Spirit that frees the sinner's will from bondage to sin and convicts, calls, illumines and enables the sinner to respond to the gospel call with repentance and faith (conversion). Calvinists and Arminians agree, against Pelagianism and semi-Pelagianism, that the sinner's will is so depraved and bound to sin

that it cannot respond positively to the gospel call without supernatural grace.[20]

Notice that Dr. Olson frames the discussion in such a way as to set up "supernatural grace" as separate from "the gospel call," as if the "graciously prevenient" work of God cannot actually be the work of the gospel itself. If I had the opportunity to press Olson on this point I would have to ask if he thinks the inspiration, dispersion, and preservation of our Scriptures is a supernatural and gracious work of God or not. If it is, then the entire Arminian premise appears to be flawed.

What must be noted is that the gospel itself meets *every* needed characteristic of this so-called "prevenient grace." Using Dr. Olson's own definition:

The *gospel* goes before, prepares the way, enables and assists the sinner's repentance and faith. (see Romans 10:14-17)

The gospel is inspired, written, carried, proclaimed and preserved by the direct action of the Holy Spirit Himself. What more must He personally do to enable the lost who hear it to respond to it? Does God's grace really need more grace to work? If so, where is that principle clearly laid out in the Scripture?

---

[20] Roger Olson, "Prevenient Grace: Why It Matters," (*Patheos*, 6/7/12). Quote taken from: https://www.pa-theos.com/blogs/rogereolson/2012/06/prevenient-grace-why-it-matters/ [date accessed: 8/15/16].

These distinctions put us beyond the scope of what most would label as *Arminian*. Nevertheless, we do share much in common with our Arminian brethren and stand with them in defense of God's love and provision for all people.

ALTERNATIVE LABELS

The labels *Non-Calvinist* or *Anti-Calvinist* fail not only because they assume an unnecessarily harsh opposition, but also because it defines one view only in relation to another. That is one reason this book has not even mentioned Calvinism up until this point. I would rather focus on the positive claims of our position rather than the negation of alternatives.

Savabilist, Extensivist, Decisionist, Conversionist and Volitionist have been suggested as alternative labels and there is much to commend each of them. They are not terms of negation, terms of modification, or terms lacking differentiation. A consensus simply has not yet formed in favor of any of these five terms. To date, the most commonly used label for a Southern Baptist who embraces the *Whosoever Will* theological tradition is clearly the term *Traditionalism*. I, however, would like to offer an alternative for consideration with the hopes to build a consensus of like-minded biblical exegetes that expands beyond the confines of our own convention...

PROVISIONISM

We believe a recognizably good God is one that *provides* for those in need.

- We are all sinners, but God *provides*.

- We cannot save ourselves, but God *provides*.

- We are hopeless, but God *provides*.

- If someone needs revelation, God *provides*.

- If someone needs atonement, God *provides*.

- If someone needs love, God *provides*.

He not only *provides* for you and me, but for every single man, woman, boy, and girl. We believe that the Bible teaches us that a good person would *provide* for those in need, and therefore God, being recognizably good, is a God who also would *provide* for all who are in need. He does not pass by His enemies on the other side of the road but stops to help just as He instructs us to do (Luke 10:25-37).

We believe that no one perishes for a lack of *provision*, but agree with Paul who said, "They perish because they refused to love the truth and so be saved" (2 Thess. 2:10). Those who end up eternally separated from God cannot rightly say, "No *provision* was made for me," or "My Creator did not really love or want me." No, they have no such excuse because they willfully rejected the sincere appeals of a gracious Father who lovingly *provided* all they needed to believe and repent so as to be saved. What better label for a soteriological worldview is there than one that highlights God's *provision* for everyone He has created?

PROVISIONISM

PEOPLE SIN
which separates all from fellowship with God.
(Rom 3:23; 6:23)

RESPONSIBLE
(able-to-respond) to God's appeals for
reconciliation .
(2 Cor 5:19-20; Jn 5:40; 12:48; 20:31; Matt 23:37)

OPEN DOOR
for anyone to enter by faith. Whosoever
will may come to his Open Arms.
(Eph 1:13; Rom 10:21; 1 Pet 3:9; 1 Tim 2:4; Jn 3:16; Matt 11:28)

VICARIOUS ATONEMENT
provides a way for anyone to be saved by
Christ's blood.
(Rom 4:5; 2 Cor 5:21; 1 Pet 3:18)

ILLUMINATING GRACE
Provides clearly revealed truth so that all
can know and respond in faith.
(Titus 2:11; Rom 1:16-2:16; 11:32; 2 Cor 4:3-6; Jn 12:32)

DESTROYED
for unbelief and resisting the Holy Spirit
(2 Thess 2:10; Jn 3:18; Acts 7:51; Rom 4:5)

ETERNAL SECURITY
for all true believers
(Rom 8:38-39; Eph 1:13-14; Jn 20:31)

SoTERIOLOGY101.COM

Appendix 2

No. Pelagius was a fifth century British monk who was accused of teaching that people had the natural ability to fulfill the commands of God by an exercise of the human will apart from divine assistance (grace). Pelagianism came to be known as the belief that mankind is born basically good, without a sinful nature, and is thus capable of doing good without God's help.[21] We deny this belief wholeheartedly.

Because Pelagius was deemed a heretic, little of his work survived to the present day except in the quotes of his opponents (not the most reliable of sources). Many modern scholars suspect that Pelagius' actual teachings were greatly misrepresented so as to demonize and marginalize him (this is not difficult to imagine).

Despite what is commonly known of Pelagius, evidence indicates that he and his followers taught that all good works come only by divine aid (grace), which was seen as "enabling," not "effectual" in nature. For instance, in a letter to the pope defending himself, Pelagius is reported to have written:

---

[21] Matt Slick, "Pelagianism," *CARM*. Quote taken from: https://carm.org/pelagianism.

This grace we for our part do not, as you suppose, allow to consist merely in the law, but also in the help of God. God helps us by His teaching and revelation, whilst He opens the eyes of our heart; whilst He points out to us the future, that we may not be absorbed in the present; whilst He discovers to us the snares of the devil; whilst He enlightens us with the manifold and ineffable gift of heavenly grace... This free will is in all good works always assisted by divine help.[22]

And in an accompanying confession of faith, he reportedly stated,

Free-will we do so own, as to say that we always stand in need of God's help... We do also abhor the blasphemy of those who say that any impossible thing is commanded to man by God; or that the commandments of God cannot be performed by any one man.

So, while Pelagius maintained human responsibility to keep the commands of God, he still seemed to maintain the need for divine aid in doing so.[23]

Augustine, a contemporary of Pelagius, was the first on record to teach the concept of individual effectual

---

[22] Gerald Bonner, "Pelagius (fl. c.390–418), theologian," *Oxford Dictionary of National Biography*, doi:10.1093/ref:odnb/21784 (Oxford University Press, 2004) [date accessed 10/28/12].

[23] Joseph Pohle, "Pelagius and Pelagianism," *The Catholic Encyclopedia*. Vol. 11. (New York: Robert Appleton Company, 1911) [date accessed: 1/18/14].

election to salvation. Loraine Boettner, a notable historian, concedes that this teaching "was first clearly seen by Augustine" in the fifth century.

Pelagius stood up against Augustine's new doctrinal positions and even went so far as to accuse him of being under the influence of his former Manichean (Gnostic) roots, which was known to teach pagan fatalism as if it were a Christian doctrine.[24] Augustine, in turn, accused Pelagius of denying any need for divine aid in the conversion process. It is likely that both of them went too far in their accusations against the other, but history reveals that it was Augustine's smears of Pelagius that won over in the court of public opinion.[25]

---

[24] "Augustine is known for a nine-year fascination with Manichaeism," Quote take from: http://blogs.record-eagle.com/?p=4705 [date accessed: 12/11/17].

"Only a handful of people in the world have read all of Augustine's extant works, and Dr. Ken Wilson may be one of only two scholars who have read the massive Augustinian collection in the order it was written (chronologically). This chronological analysis exposed that 'Augustine departed from what the earliest church fathers believed about people's freedom to choose God,' says Wilson. 'The early church did not view God as deterministic, but Augustine changed that by combining Christianity with Gnostic Manichaeism, Stoicism, and Neoplatonism.' Because of Augustine's immersion in Greek philosophy (Stoicism and Neoplatonism) and Gnostic Manichaeism, his version of Christianity became deterministic – everything is unilaterally predetermined by God." Ken Wilson, *Augustine's Conversion from Traditional Free Choice to 'Non-free Free Will': A Comprehensive Methodology* (Mohr Seibeck, 2018).

[25] The determination of the Council of Orange (529) could be considered "semi-Augustinian." It defined that faith, though a free act, resulted even in its beginnings from the grace of God, enlightening the human mind and enabling belief. However, it also explicitly denied double predestination (of the equal-ultimacy variety), stating, "We not only do not believe that any are foreordained to evil by the power of God, but

Pelagianism, whether accurately or not, has become known historically as "the teaching that man has the capacity to seek God in and of himself apart from any movement of God or the Holy Spirit, and therefore that salvation is affected by man's efforts."[26] I deny this belief and consider the label offensive and completely misrepresentative of our actual teachings (and I am under the impression Pelagius himself would express similar sentiments if given a fair hearing today).

Below I have listed a few reasons why this label would not rightly represent our views:

1. We believe man has the capacity to respond willingly to God's means of seeking to save the lost, not that man would seek God if left completely alone without any help.

2. We believe our gracious God is actively working in and through creation, conscience, His Bride,

---

even state with utter abhorrence that if there are those who want to believe so evil a thing, they are anathema." The document links grace with baptism, which was not a controversial subject at the time. It received papal sanction. [Francis Oakley, *The Medieval Experience: Foundations of Western Cultural Singularity*, (Toronto: University of Toronto Press, 1988) 64.; Don Thorsen, *An Exploration of Christian Theology*, (Grand Rapids: Baker Academic, 2007) 20.3.4.; Cf. Second Council of Orange ch.5-7.; H.J. Denzinger, *Enchiridion Symbolorum et Definitionum*, 375-377; C. H. Pickar, (1981) [1967], "Faith", *The New Catholic Encyclopedia* v. 5 (Thompson/Gale: Detroit, MI and Washington D.C., 2003) 797; *The Oxford Dictionary of the Christian Church*, edited by F. L. Cross and E. A. Livingstone, (New York: Oxford University Press, 2005).

[26] Nicholas Adams, "Pelagianism: Can people be saved by their own efforts?" *Heresies and How to Avoid Them*, edited by Ben Quash and Ward, Michael (London: SPCK Publishing, 2007), 91.

His Holy Spirit-filled followers, and His Word to aid humanity in their conversion.

3. We believe salvation is wholly of God in that He owes no man forgiveness or eternal life, even if they freely repent and humbly submit to Him as Lord and Savior. Asking for forgiveness no more merits that forgiveness than the prodigal son's return home merited the reception he received from his father. That was the choice of a gracious father alone.

ARE YOU TEACHING SEMI-PELAGIANISM?

No. This is another man-made term used to associate one's theological opponents with known heretical figures of the past. For instance, Broughton Knox accused another Christian scholar, Howard Marshall, of being a "Semi-Pelagian" by stating,

The Pelagian mind is inclined to ascribe, shall we say, 5% to God and 95% to man, the semi-Pelagian 50%-50%, while the evangelical Arminian, such as our writer, 95% to God and 5% to man. Yet, after all, it is this last 5% which makes the difference between heaven and hell, so that man is, in the end, his own saviour.

I must ask this vital question: What exactly are these percentages representing? "Semi-Pelagians" are supposedly ascribing 95% of what to God?

95% of man's desires?

95% of man's sin?

95% of man's choices?

95% of Christ's provision of atonement?

95% of salvation?

95% of WHAT!?!

It seems to me that in the well-meant effort of some theologians to ascribe all good things to God they have unintentionally also ascribed all bad things to Him, even if only by implication. So, while Knox seems most concerned with making sure mankind takes no credit for their salvation, Marshall seems more concerned with a recognizably good and Holy God. I suspect both men have a noble purpose in their pursuits, but as with most disputes the balance is somewhere in the middle. This balance, however, cannot be seen in dividing vaguely defined percentages of what is to be ascribed to God and to man.

We firmly and unequivocally believe that salvation is 100% of God. Merely affirming the responsibility of mankind to accept and/or reject God's appeals for reconciliation does not in any way affect that percentage.

Only when a theological opponent, like Knox in the quote above, conflates man's choice to humbly repent in faith with God's choice to save whosoever does so are these types of dilemmas created. In other words, Knox has created a dilemma by conflating two choices as if they were one and calling them both "salvation."

For instance, the prodigal son's choice to return home is distinct from the father's choice to redeem him once he arrives. To treat those two distinct choices as if they were one and the same (i.e., under the meticulous control of the father) creates an unnecessary dilemma.

Likewise, a sinner's choice to repent in response to God's appeals for reconciliation is distinct from God's choice to provide those means of reconciliation through Christ's blood. Thus, God is always the decisive cause of whom He saves and the means by which He saves them. And mankind is the decisive cause of his own sin and his choice to repent of it. Only by conflating these two distinct choices is this dilemma created. God is 100% responsible for his choices. Man is 100% responsible for his choices. There is no dilemma here.

WHY WE ARE NOT SEMI-PELAGIAN

In a lengthy discussion with notable Apologist and founder of CARM ministries, Matt Slick, over our soteriological differences, he more than once accused me of "Semi-Pelagianism." Here is how Matt describes Semi-Pelagianism on his popular website:

Semi-Pelagianism is a weaker form of Pelagianism (a heresy derived from Pelagius who lived in the 5th century A.D. and was a teacher in Rome). Semi-Pelagianism (advocated by Cassian at Marseilles, 5th

Century)[27] did not deny original sin and its effects upon the human soul and will, but it taught that God and man cooperate to achieve man's salvation. This cooperation is not by human effort as in keeping the law but rather in the ability of a person to make a free will choice. The semi-Pelagian teaches that man can make the first move toward God by seeking God out of his own free will and that man can cooperate with God's grace even to the keeping of his faith through human effort. This would mean that God responds to the initial effort of a person and that God's grace is not absolutely necessary to maintain faith.[28]

First, have I ever affirmed that "God and man cooperate to achieve man's salvation?" Of course not! Let me clarify this point of contention by once again asking a question: Did the prodigal son and his father cooperate to achieve the son's restoration, or was that a gracious choice of the father alone upon his son's

---

[27] The view that Cassian propounded Semi-Pelagianism has been disputed. Lauren Pristas writes: "For Cassian, salvation is, from beginning to end, the effect of God's grace. It is fully divine. Salvation, however, is salvation of a rational creature who has sinned through free choice. Therefore, salvation necessarily includes both free human consent in grace and the gradual rehabilitation in grace of the faculty of free choice. Thus Cassian insists salvation is also fully human. His thought, however, is not Semi-Pelagian, nor do readers who submit to the whole corpus emerge Semi-Pelagians." Lauren Pristas, *The Theological Anthropology of John Cassian.* 1993. Boston College, PhD dissertation. *WorldCat*, https://www.worldcat.org/title/theological-anthropology-of-john-cassian/oclc/39451854&referer=brief_results.

[28] Matt Slick, "Semi-Pelagianism," *CARM*. Quote taken from: https://carm.org/semi-pelagianism [date accessed 9/7/17].

return? The false belief that forgiveness is somehow owed to those who freely humble themselves and ask for it leads to erroneous conflations such as this.

Second, have I ever affirmed that "man can make the first move toward God by seeking God out of his own free will?" Absolutely not! Mankind's ability to respond willingly to God's gracious revelation is not equal to mankind's ability to seek and find a transcendent God who remains distant and unknowable. How will they believe in one whom they have not heard (Rom. 10:14)?

Third, have we ever affirmed that "God responds to the initial effort of a person?" No! Belief that mankind is able to willingly respond to the gracious means of God to seek and save the lost is not equal to mankind making "the first move toward God."

If it was proven that I could not call the President of the United States on the phone, would you also conclude, based on that information, that it would be impossible for me to answer the phone if the President tried to call me? Of course not, but that is exactly what those who accuse me of Semi-Pelagianism are doing.

THE BOOGIE-MAN FALLACY

In Matt's short-sighted and ill-informed effort to discredit my perspective, he resorted to what is known as a "boogie-man fallacy." This is a certain type of argument which, in fact, is not an argument, but a means of forestalling discussion and erroneously labelling an opponent's position with that of a known heresy so as to demonize and discredit it.

For example, someone in a debate might say, "Look! His view sounds like something Hitler said, so you shouldn't listen to him anymore." Hitler is a known "boogie-man" or "bad character," so if I can associate my opponent's views with Hitler, then I'll discredit him all together. Likewise, Pelagius has become some theological opponents go-to "boogie man," and many of them will stop at nothing to slap that label on me so as to marginalize and discredit anything I say.

This method bears a certain resemblance to the ad hominem fallacy, and comes from the same root motivation: discredit and marginalize the person and their views rather than objectively evaluating and offering a sound, non-fallacious biblical rebuttal.

The ad hominem fallacy consists of attempting to refute an argument by impeaching the character of its proponent, whereas the boogie-man fallacy seeks to associate an argument with that of someone whose character (or belief) has already been impeached (like poor ol' Pelagius).

This is pure "guilt by association" and it is the lazy man's approach to avoid an otherwise rational and informed discussion of the issues. Those who resort to such tactics either do not know any better or they are nefariously attempting to marginalize and demonize the views of those who disagree with them. Readers of this book can no longer appeal to the former as an excuse.

If those who affirm libertarian free will can rightly be labeled "Semi-Pelagian," then by that standard we could conclude that theistic determinists are "Semi-Gnostic;" after all, those were the two groups promoting the extremes of both views in the fourth and fifth centuries when such labels were originated.

I would rather avoid such demonizing labels altogether and actually practice the principle of *sola scriptura* (Scripture alone). Rather than appealing to ancient Catholic labels created by men who were known for their often violent and extreme intolerance of dissenting views, how about we approach each other with patience, kindness and the principle of charity? Let us not repeat the mistakes of those who lead the church into the Inquisition and other horrific abuses of dissenters, but instead set a better example for theological discourse to all who come after us.[29]

---

[29] For further study on this topic I highly recommend an article by Dr. David Allen titled, "Claims, Clarity, Charity – Why the Traditional Baptist Statement on Soteriology is not and cannot be Semipelagian," published on Oct. 1, 2018 and can be found at www.drdavidlallen.com.

Appendix 3

A common objection against my theological perspective is that it "exalts mankind" because it maintains mankind's moral ability-to-respond (responsibility) to God's appeals. I regularly hear the accusation that my view somehow "steals God's glory by exalting humanity," but is this a fair accusation? Let's objectively examine the natural (lost/un-regenerate) man to see if I really teach a "lower" view of the natural condition of humanity.

Which view of man is lower, the one that maintains his ability to believe and repent in light of the gospel, or one that teaches he is born in a condition that cannot willingly respond to God's appeals? Which person is more worthy of blame, the one who innately hates and rejects a God who first hated and rejected him, or the one who freely chooses to hate and reject a God who first loved and provided for him?

One can only feel pity for people born in a condition beyond their control which irrevocably causes them to always rebel and reject God's gracious appeals. They are born, in a sense, victims of God's eternal decree and without hope of salvation. The only thing more devastating than a lost soul is a lost soul without anyone looking for her or providing her hope of being found.

The good news is that our God is good! Because He is good we know that no child is born unloved by their Creator, rejected by their Maker, or unwanted by their God. Every life matters because God created all people in His own image. Any doctrine which undermines this truth, even if unintentionally, should be firmly rejected and openly rebutted.

In 1 John 4:8 we are told, "God is love." And the Psalmist said, "The Lord is gracious and merciful; Slow to anger and great in lovingkindness. The Lord is good to all, And His mercies are over all His works" (Ps. 145:8-9). The apostle Peter put it this way: "The Lord is not slow in keeping his promise, as some understand slowness. Instead he is patient with you, not wanting anyone to perish, but everyone to come to repentance" (2 Peter 3:9). And Paul, under inspiration, stated it like this, "This is good, and pleases God our Savior, who wants all people to be saved and to come to a knowledge of the truth. For there is one God and one mediator between God and mankind, the man Christ Jesus, who gave himself as a ransom for all people. This has now been witnessed to at the proper time" (1 Tim. 2:3-6).

Our God loves and wants the aborted, abandoned and unwanted children of this earth. He saves the weak and humble because He is gracious and kind (Ps. 18:27).

INNOCENT BY REASON OF INSANITY

Consider those who are deemed clinically insane in our own judicial system. The unfortunate people born with mental illness who literally cannot control their behaviors due to tumors, chemical imbalances or other similar ailments may be declared "insane" and hospitalized, but our judicial system still recognizes their "innocence" due to their incapacities. The court's ruling of "innocent by reason of insanity" relates to this contrast because it illustrates the true nature of what makes a man responsible and thus blameworthy.

This also relates to how we view God, the judge. How do you feel about a judge who sends a mentally ill criminal to the electric chair for committing a crime that he literally could not have refrained from committing due to factors beyond his control? How do you view that criminal? In this scenario the judge is painted in a very bad light and the criminal is seen as a victim of sorts. In contrast, if the criminal is shown to have committed a premeditated crime with malice and full responsibility as a sane person, the judge seems much more just (praiseworthy) and the criminal far more guilty (blameworthy).

For this reason, a good district attorney seeking a guilty conviction would vehemently argue that the defendant was of "sound mind" and "had the capacity to refrain from the criminal behavior" for which he stands trial. So too, we stand to make a parallel argument against all unbelievers who end up in Hell.

The lost unbeliever cannot resort to the defense of "Total Inability." Those perishing in Hell cannot rightly say, "I was born hated and rejected by my Maker, unable to choose otherwise," or "The revelation of God, even the powerful truth of the gospel, was insufficient to enable me to willingly respond in faith." The lost do not have any excuses for their unbelief (Rom. 1:20). And I cannot think of any better excuse than that provided by the teaching of some theologians regarding the incapacity of man's nature to respond willingly to God Himself.

Unbelievers are guilty of unbelief because it is their responsibility (read "ability-to-respond") to believe God's gracious and abundantly clear revelation. To remove that ability (moral or otherwise) is to undermine their guilt and God's justice.

God has graciously granted all people the ability to respond to His clearly revealed truth and then judges them for their choice to rebel or repent in light of Christ's word (see John 12:47-48).

Those who perish only perish "because they refused to love the truth so as to be saved" (2 Thess. 2:10). The lost cannot claim they were rejected by their own Maker before they were born. They cannot say they were unloved or not provided what was necessary to believe and be saved! They were not born haters of God who could not have chosen to do otherwise because of a divine unchangeable decree prior to the creation of the world.

These are not new arguments, by any means. In fact, in the first and second century we have record of the Earliest Church Fathers making this same case:

Irenaeus (AD 120-202):

(Irenaeus was a student of Polycarp, who in turn was traditionally known to be a disciple of John the Evangelist.)

God therefore has given that which is good, as the apostle tells us in this Epistle, and they who work it shall receive glory and honor, because they have done that which is good when they had it in their power not to do it; but those who do it not shall receive the just judgment of God, because they did not work good when they had it in their power so to do.

But if some had been made by nature bad, and others good, these latter would not be deserving of praise for being good, for such were they created; nor would the former be reprehensible, for thus they were made [originally]. But since all men are of the same nature, able both to hold fast and to do what is good; and, on the other hand, having also the power to cast it from them and not to do it, — some do justly receive praise even among men who are under the control of good laws (and much more from God), and obtain deserved testimony of their choice of good in general, and of persevering therein; but the others are blamed, and receive a just condemnation, because of their rejection of what is fair and good. And therefore the prophets used to exhort men to what was good, to act justly and to work righteousness, as I have so largely demonstrated, because it is in our power so to do, and because by excessive negligence we might become forgetful, and thus stand in need of that good counsel which the good God has given us to know by means of the prophets... No doubt, if anyone is unwilling to follow the Gospel itself, it is in his power [to reject it], but it is not expedient. For it is in man's power to disobey God, and to forfeit what is good; but [such conduct] brings no small amount of injury and mischief... But because man is possessed of free will from the beginning, and God is possessed of free will, in whose likeness man was created, advice is always given to him to keep fast the good, which thing is done by means of obedience to God.[30]

Justin Martyr (AD 110-165)

But lest some suppose, from what has been said by us, that we say that whatever happens, happens by a fatal necessity, because it is foretold as known beforehand, this too we explain. We have learned from the prophets, and we hold it to be true, that

---

[30] Irenaeus, *Against Heresies*, Bk. IV, 37.

punishments, and chastisements, and good rewards, are rendered according to the merit of each man's actions. Since if it be not so, but all things happen by fate, neither is anything at all in our own power. For if it be fated that this man, e.g., be good, and this other evil, neither is the former meritorious nor the latter to be blamed. And again, unless the human race have the power of avoiding evil and choosing good by free choice, they are not accountable for their actions, of whatever kind they be. But that it is by free choice they both walk uprightly and stumble, we thus demonstrate. We see the same man making a transition to opposite things. Now, if it had been fated that he were to be either good or bad, he could never have been capable of both the opposites, nor of so many transitions. But not even would some be good and others bad, since we thus make fate the cause of evil, and exhibit her as acting in opposition to herself; or that which has been already stated would seem to be true, that neither virtue nor vice is anything, but that things are only reckoned good or evil by opinion; which, as the true word shows, is the greatest impiety and wickedness. But this we assert is inevitable fate, that they who choose the good have worthy rewards, and they who choose the opposite have their merited awards. For not like other things, as trees and quadrupeds, which cannot act by choice, did God make man: for neither would

145

he be worthy of reward or praise did he not of himself choose the good, but were created for this end; nor, if he were evil, would he be worthy of punishment, not being evil of himself, but being able to be nothing else than what he was made.[31]

Tertullian (AD 145-220)

In order, therefore, that man might have a goodness of his own, bestowed on him by God, and there might be henceforth in man a property, and in a certain sense a natural attribute of goodness, there was assigned to him in the constitution of his nature, as a formal witness of the goodness which God bestowed upon him, freedom and power of the will, such as should cause good to be performed spontaneously by man, as a property of his own, on the ground that no less than this would be required in the matter of a goodness which was to be voluntarily exercised by him, that is to say, by the liberty of his will, without either favor or servility to the constitution of his nature, so that man should be good just up to this point, if he should display his goodness in accordance with his natural constitution indeed, but still as the result of his will, as a property of his nature; and, by a similar exercise of volition, should show himself to be too strong in defense against evil also (for even this God, of course, foresaw), being free, and master of himself;

---

[31] Justin, *First Apology*, XLIII.

because, if he were wanting in this prerogative of self-mastery, so as to perform even good by necessity and not will, he would, in the helplessness of his servitude, become subject to the usurpation of evil, a slave as much to evil as to good. Entire freedom of will, therefore, was conferred upon him in both tendencies; so that, as master of himself, he might constantly encounter good by spontaneous observance of it, and evil by its spontaneous avoidance; because, were man even otherwise circumstanced, it was yet his bounden duty, in the judgment of God, to do justice according to the motions of his will regarded, of course, as free. But the reward neither of good nor of evil could be paid to the man who should be found to have been either good or evil through necessity and not choice. In this really lay the law which did not exclude, but rather prove, human liberty by a spontaneous rendering of obedience, or a spontaneous commission of iniquity; so patent was the liberty of man's will for either issue. Since, therefore, both the goodness and purpose of God are discovered in the gift to man of freedom in his will, it is not right, after ignoring the original definition of goodness and purpose which it was necessary to determine previous to any discussion of the subject, on subsequent facts to presume to say that God ought not in such a way to have formed man, because the issue was other than what was assumed to be proper for God. We ought rather, after duly considering that it behooved God so to create man, to leave this consideration unimpaired, and to survey the other aspects of the case. It is, no doubt, an easy process for persons who take offence at the fall of man, before they have looked into the facts of his creation, to impute the blame of what happened to the Creator, without any examination of His purpose. To conclude: the goodness of God, then fully considered from the beginning of His works, will be enough to convince us that nothing evil could possibly have come forth from God; and the liberty of man will, after a second thought, show us that it alone is chargeable with the fault which itself committed.[32]

---

[32] Tertullian, *Against Marcion*, Bk. II, Ch. VI.

Appendix 4

Some new to *Traditionalism* (or *Provisionism*) ask if I am promoting "inclusivism." Like most labels, there are various ways in which this can be understood. Some have wrongly come to understand inclusivism as meaning that all roads (religions) lead us to God and salvation, so it really does not matter if you believe in Jesus or some other deity as long as you are sincere.

First, this belief is called "pluralism," not "inclusivism," and it should be quite obvious that I completely and whole-heartedly reject such teachings.

Second, it should be noted that there are a variety of views among inclusivists. Charles Pinnock, one of the leading voices, affirms that salvation is found only through Jesus Christ while maintaining that God intends his salvation to be available to all humans everywhere. With this point we are in absolute agreement. Where we may find some disagreement is regarding the necessity of hearing and responding to the specific revelation about Jesus for salvation at this current time.

We would say salvation is *exclusively* by the gospel, and anyone that obeys the gospel (which comes by faith) is *inclusively* put in Christ (i.e., covered by the work of Jesus on the cross). This has been the same gospel since the beginning. No one, from Adam, until the Lord returns, has ever been saved outside of the gospel.

As explained in more detail earlier, the gospel is not limited to specific knowledge of Jesus and His work on the cross, but also involves God's very character and His provision for all people at all times. In order to obey the gospel, you do not have to know all the specifics about the life and work of Jesus. The specific truth of Christ and His work explains why we have had a gospel available to us since the beginning. That is how God justifies us through the gospel, the good news about the love and provision of our Creator. Christ and His work is the fullness and cornerstone of the gospel.

If anyone believes that specific knowledge of Jesus and His work on the cross is necessary for salvation at all times and in all places, they will have issues with:

1. Every Old Testament believer

2. All the NT believers before Jesus died on the cross and was raised, to include people like:

    a. John the Baptist's parents (Zacharias and Elizabeth who were "righteous" before God)

    b. Mary the mother of Jesus

    c. Simeon of the temple (Luke 2:25)

d. John the Baptist

e. The Apostles

All of them were described as "righteous" (credited of course). How? They believed the truth they were told and God graciously credited them with the righteousness provided by Christ, who they did not yet know. They repented and trusted in the Lord for their salvation. None of them, however, knew that Jesus was going to die and be raised from the dead. There may be a few in the OT that had some inkling that the Messiah would die, but Scripture is pretty clear that these specifics were hidden and remained a mystery (1 Cor. 2:7; Eph. 3:1-9). We know for certain that the disciples did not know and understand this, and they preached the gospel (before the cross), and I do not think anyone would say they were not "credited with righteousness" prior to Christ's resurrection.

We hold that it has always been the Son of God interacting with man since the beginning. Those who were trusting in "God" in the OT were actually trusting in the Son. John 1:9-13 tells us that the Son of God has been, since the beginning, in the world enlightening every man (of the gospel), and that those who receive Him through faith He gave the right to become children of God. Notice the next verse, John 1:14: "and then the Word became flesh."

Christ is the Lord of all, and has always been the Lord. The Son has always been the intermediary of man to the Father. The Son has always been the One reconciling us to the Father (2 Cor. 5:19). So, when Abraham believed God, and it was credited to Him as righteousness, Abraham was trusting in the One who the Father sent; he was trusting in the Son. By obeying the gospel, Abraham was put into Christ's work on the cross, though he likely was not aware of all the details. He was in Christ, and by being in Christ, Abraham produced the fruit of righteousness that can only come by being in Christ.

Consider Jesus' teaching in John 15:1-11 regarding the vine, branches and its fruit. This is before the cross. Christ says that you can only be righteous and produce righteous fruit if you abide in Him. He tells the disciples (again who don't know of His death and resurrection) that they are already "abiding in Him" and are already "clean" (John 15:3).

They repented and trusted in the Lord for their salvation, and were credited with the work that Jesus would do on the cross. Paul teaches this in Romans 3:21-26, saying that we are justified by faith, based on the faithfulness of the Son. Paul says even Abraham was justified by faith, based on the cross in the fourth chapter of Romans.

In conclusion, let me be abundantly clear about this question by clearly laying out what *we do not believe*:

- That all will be saved; that is universalism.

- That anyone is saved outside of the gospel.

- That you can know of Christ and reject Him and be saved.

- That you can, by works, earn righteousness and be saved.

- That all religions lead to Christ.

Appendix 5

I
f I tell my child that he should clean his room it does strongly imply that he could clean his room. This is basic common sense, but is it applicable to how God deals with humanity? Is the implication in scripture of "you should" mean that "you could?"

I think we can all agree that "ought" strongly implies moral ability for all practical purposes, but is that a biblical reality in every instance? Sometimes the Bible defies our practical sensibilities and turns our reality upon its ear. Is that the case here? Do God's expressions of what we *should* do imply that we actually *could* do it.[33]

CONSIDER THIS ANALOGY

Suppose you had a horrible gambling addiction and as a result accrued a debt so large that it was literally impossible for you to repay. Would your inability to pay

---

[33] Norman Geisler summarizes the problem in this way: "If I'm really not the cause of my actions, why should I take responsibility for them? Why should I take either credit or blame? After all, the extreme Calvinists believes that ought does not imply can. Responsibility does not imply the ability to respond. If this is so, why should I feel responsible? Why should I care when it's completely out of my hand one way or the other?" Norman L. Geisler, Chosen But Free: A Balanced View of God's Sovereignty and Free Will, 3rd ed. (Minneapolis: Bethany House, 2010), 13.

off this debt excuse you from paying it? Of course not. You *should* pay off this debt regardless of whether or not you *could* pay off this debt. This is an example of where inability does not remove responsibility and thus *should* does not mean that one necessarily *could*.

Likewise, the scriptures teach us that we *should* obey the law of God perfectly (Matt. 5:48), but it also teaches us that no one *could* (Rom. 3:23). Our moral inability to fulfill the law's demands does not remove our moral responsibility to the law. We have a sin debt that we cannot pay, yet scripture seems to teach that we are held accountable for that debt nonetheless. In this instance, it certainly does seem that *should* does not imply *could*.

But, continuing with the analogy above, suppose your wealthy and benevolent father offered to pay your gambling debt for you if you would confess your addiction and go to rehab. Clearly, this is something you *should* do, but *could* you? Of course, you could! Your inability to pay off the debt in no way hinders you from accepting the benevolent offer of your father's provision.

Likewise, with regard to the law, your benevolent and gracious Father offers to pay your sin debt if you confess your sin addiction and trust in Him. Clearly, this is something you *should* do, but *could* you? Of course, you *could!* Your inability to pay off your sin debt in no way hinders you from accepting the benevolent offer of your Father's gracious provision.

Suppose someone tried to convince you that one's inability to pay off their debt equaled their inability to accept help when it was offered. Would you believe them? I ask because that is what some are attempting to get the church to believe. Allow me to explain further.

Could the "Rich Young Ruler" have willingly given up his wealth to follow Christ as Zacchaeus does in the very next chapter? Or was Zacchaeus granted an ability that was withheld from the Rich Young Ruler?[34]

All theologians agree that they both *should* have given up everything to follow Christ, but only some of us maintains that both of them *could* have willingly done so. Why do some insist that *should* doesn't imply *could* when it comes to the Biblical revelation?

Dr. Wayne Grudem explains the issue in this manner:

> Advocates of the Arminian position draw attention to the frequency of the free offer of the gospel in the New Testament. They would say that these invitations to people to repent and come to Christ for salvation, if bona fide, must imply the ability to respond to them. Thus, all people without exception

---

[34] I'm speaking of man's moral/spiritual abilities to repent in faith, not their physical ability or mental assent, so please do not dismiss this point with the all too often rebuttal of, "He is able but not willing." If one's nature is such that they cannot will to do other than what God has decreed for them to do, then the point is the same regardless of the semantics.

have the ability to respond, not just those who have been sovereignly given that ability by God in a special way.[35]

Grudem, like John Hendryx of mongerism.com, rebuts this perspective by making arguments such as:

What the Scriptures say we 'ought' to do does not necessarily imply what we 'can' do. The Ten Commandments, likewise, speak of what we ought to do but they do not imply that we have the moral ability to carry them out. The law of God was given so that we would be stripped of having any hope from ourselves. Even faith itself is a divine command that we cannot fulfill without the application of God's regenerative grace by the Holy Spirit.[36]

Are you following this argument? Here it is put very simply:

1. God tells man they *should* keep all the commandments.

2. Man *cannot* keep all the commandments.

3. God also tells man they *should* believe and repent for breaking commandments.

---

[35] Wayne A. Grudem, *Systematic Theology: An Introduction to Biblical Doctrine*, (Grand Rapids: Zondervan, 1994), 341.

[36] John Hendryx, *What Do Arminianism and Hyper-Calvinism Share in Common?* Quote take from: https://www.monergism.com/thethreshold/articles/onsite/HyperArmin.html [date accessed: 1/5/18].

4.   Therefore man also *cannot* believe and repent for breaking commandments.[37]

If the fallacy in this argument is not obvious to you, please allow me to use the analogy above as a parallel:

1.   The gambler *should* pay off his gambling debts.

2.   The gambler *cannot* pay off his gambling debts.

3.   The father tells the man he *should* admit his addiction and receive help.

4.   Therefore the gambler *cannot* admit his addiction and receive help.

Maybe another analogy will help bring more clarity: Back when my kids were younger we did a family activity

---

[37] Obligation Objection: Simply put, ought implies can and moral duties make no sense in compatibilism. 1 Cor. 10.13 can be cited as an example for libertarian freedom (God gives a way out of sin, yet we still sin). Prevenient grace seems to be a legitimate postulation, that is, the grace that precedes salvation that enables one to repent and turn from sin. Their example: P is "we ought to avoid all sin," and Q is "we can avoid all sin" (ought implies can). However, it seems that some theologies (mainly Reformed), after the fall, P is true and Q is false (counterexample?). How about: P1, For any x, if x is a sin, then we ought to avoid doing x; Q1 For any x, if x is a sin, then we can avoid x. Here is where David Baggett and Jerry Walls (Arminians) show the Calvinist's fallacy of equivocation. Clearly, P1 and Q2 are true but to understand where P is true and Q is false one would need to equivocate "all" for P as "for each individual sin x, taken on its own" and for Q "for the sum total of all sins added together." An argument on equivocation seems to break at the seams. Thus, the principle of ought implies can perseveres and libertarian freedom is true. Quote taken from: http://sententias.org/2013/04/22/qa-19/ [date accessed 2/4/18].

that our church had suggested. I stood at the top of the stairs with my four children at the bottom.

I said to them, "Here are the rules. You must get from the bottom of the stairs to the top of the stairs without touching any of the railing, the wall or even the stairs. Ready, go!"

My kids looked at me and then each other and then back at their mother. With bewilderment in their eyes, they immediately began to whine and complain saying, "Dad, that is impossible!" I told them to stop whining and figure it out.

The youngest stood at the bottom and started trying to jump, slamming himself into the steps over and over. The more creative one of the bunch began looking for tools to help build some kind of contraption. Another set down on the floor while loudly declaring, "This is just stupid, no one can do that!"

Finally, in exasperation one of the kids yelled out, "Dad, why don't you just help us?" I raised my eyebrows as if to give them a clue that they may be on the right track. The eldest caught on quickly.

"Can you help us dad?" he shouted.

I replied quietly, "No one even asked me."

"Can you carry us up the stairs?" he asked.

"I will if you ask me," I said. And one by one, I carried each child to the top after they simply asked.

Then, we sat down and talked about salvation. We talked about how it is impossible for us to get to heaven by our own efforts, but if we ask Christ for help then He will carry us. It was a great visual lesson of God's grace in contrast with man's works.

But suppose that my children's inability to get to the top the stairs also meant they were incapable of asking me for help. Imagine how this story would've played out if it was impossible for my children not only to get to the top of the stairs but equally impossible for them to recognize that inability and receive help when it was offered.

This illustrates the mistake of some theologians. Let's go back to the fallacy above as it relates to my story:

1. Dad tells his kids they *should* get to the top of stairs.

2. Kids *cannot* complete this task as requested.

3. Dad also tells the kids they *should* receive the help he offers.

4. Therefore the kids *cannot* receive help when offered.

Do you see the problem now? The whole purpose of presenting my kids with that dilemma was to help them to discover their need for help. To suggest that they cannot realize their need and ask for help on the basis that they cannot get to the top of the stairs completely undermines the very purpose of giving them that dilemma in the first place.

The purpose of the father in both instances is to get others to trust Him. The law was not sent for the purpose of getting mankind to heaven. Just as the purpose of the activity was not to get the kids to the top of the staircase. The purpose was to help them to see that they have a need and that they cannot do it on their own.

Some theologians have wrongly concluded that because mankind is unable to attain righteousness by works through the law, they must also be equally unable to attain righteousness by grace through faith. In other words, they have concluded that because mankind is incapable of "making it to the top of the stairs," then they are equally incapable of "recognizing their inability and receiving help." This simply does not follow and it is not biblical. Paul said;

> **Romans 9:30-32:** What then shall we say? That the Gentiles, who did not pursue righteousness, have obtained it, a righteousness that is by faith; but the people of Israel, who pursued the law as the way of righteousness, have not attained their goal. Why not? Because they pursued it not by faith but as if it were by works.

Are we to believe that because pursuit by works fails in attaining righteousness that a pursuit by faith would not even be possible? Of course not. This is simply never taught in scripture.

When some theologians are pressed on the obvious implication that *should* implies *could*, they appeal to the demands of the law, which is like appealing to my demands for the children to get to the top of the stairs without touching anything. I didn't make that demand with the expectation of my children actually doing it, after all, it is impossible. I made the demand to help them realize they could not do it without my help.

So too, God did not send the law with the expectation that we could actually fulfill its demands. That is not the purpose of the law. According to the scripture, "No one will be declared righteous in God's sight by the works of the law; rather, through the law we become conscious of our sin" (Rom. 3:20).

The law is a "tutor" who points us to our need for Christ (Gal. 3:24). The law was never sent for the purpose of being fulfilled by mankind, just as the stair-climbing activity was never intended to be completed by my kids. It was a "tutoring" lesson to teach my children that they must rely on someone else, a useless activity indeed if they are somehow incapable of coming to that realization or admitting their need for help.

If my kids are as completely incapable of understanding their need for help in getting to the top of stairs as they are in getting to the top of the stairs without help, then why would I bother with the activity in the first place? Likewise, if mankind is as completely incapable of trusting in the One who fulfilled the law as they are in fulfilling the law themselves, then what is the point in sending an insufficient tutor to teach them a lesson they cannot learn?

The argument that *should* implies *could* remains virtually unanswered by those theologians who appeal to the law as their example. That is, unless they can demonstrate that it actually was God's intention for us to fulfill the law's demand in order to attain righteousness. After all, to conclude that man cannot, by any means, fulfill the purpose of the law's demands begs the question, because it presumes man cannot fulfill the purpose of the law by believing in the One who fulfilled its demands.

Basic common sense tells us that if one ought to do something, he can do it. This is especially true if one is punished for his failure to do that which is expected. In 2 Thessalonians 2:10, Paul says of the unrighteous, "They perish because they did not accept the love of the truth in order to be saved." And in John 12:48, Jesus said, "There is a judge for the one who rejects me and does not accept my words; the very words I have spoken will condemn them at the last day."

Scripture never once says that we will perish because of Adam's sin. But over and over again it says that we will each be held accountable for our response to the clear the revelation of God.[38]

---

[38] Adam Harwood explains, "Those who claim that infants inherit sin and guilt are faced with the following inconsistencies in their viewpoint: First, it would be inconsistent for God to hold infants guilty of the sin of another person (Adam) because he states that he holds people responsible for their own sin, not the for sin of another person (Ezek. 18:20). Each of us will give an account of himself to God (Rom. 14:12). We will not give an account to God of our parents or grandparents or even our furthest descendants, Adam. Second, because the Scriptures indicate that God judges people for their sinful thoughts, attitudes, and actions, it would be inconsistent for him to judge infants to be guilty of sin solely based on their sin nature." Adam Harwood, *The Spiritual Condition of Infants: A Biblical-Historical Survey and Systematic Proposal* (Eugene, OR: Wipf & Stock, 2011), 159.

$1\frac{1}{4}$

$1\_$ 3.20

$\frac{1}{4}$ .80

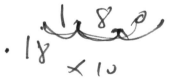

$.18 \times 10$

Printed in Great Britain
by Amazon